# THE CHRISTIAN FAMILY WORKBOOK

# THE CHRISTIAN FAMILY WORKBOOK

### PASTOR LORETTA RORIE

authorHOUSE®

*AuthorHouse™*
*1663 Liberty Drive*
*Bloomington, IN 47403*
*www.authorhouse.com*
*Phone: 1-800-839-8640*

*First published by AuthorHouse    10/20/2011*

*ISBN: 978-1-4567-9970-0 (sc)*
*ISBN: 978-1-4567-9969-4 (ebk)*

*Library of Congress Control Number: 2011915833*

*Printed in the United States of America*

*Any people depicted in stock imagery provided by Thinkstock are models, and such images are being used for illustrative purposes only.*
*Certain stock imagery © Thinkstock.*

*This book is printed on acid-free paper.*

# CONTENTS

## ACKNOWLEDGEMENTS

I would like to first of all thank my heavenly Father. I thank Him for His Son Jesus. I thank Him for the Blood of Jesus that gives me strength from day to day to keep on going in His name. I thank God for every mountain as well as every valley. Approximately five years ago I started a Bible Class on a teleconference line. We met and still meet every Thursday evening.

We had people on the teleconference line from various states. Some lessons I would mail out, some I would e-mail and others I would hand deliver at church. I had to get these lessons out in a timely fashion so that we could all come together on the following Thursday. Well this book is 52 of the 80 lessons that we studied.

Since the Bible Class teleconference line has been in existence some have came and some have gone. I would like to give a special thanks to those who have started out with me and the Bible Class and have been faithful. Special Thanks to **Sis. Mattie Kelley of Jamaica, New York, Bro. Charles Martin of Hollis, New York,** and **Sis. Diane Gary of Chgo, Il.**. I want to say Thank You again to **Sis. Janice Posey of Lockport, Il., Evang. Gloria Pfeiffer of Glendale, Az**. and **Sis. Dorothy Scruggs of Columbus, Ohio.** These are those that kept me inspired to do every lesson. Thanks to all of you and may God bless each and every one of you for your faithfulness.

## MUCH LOVE AND THANKS

Pastor Rorie, would like to give special thanks to her church family, **Prayer Is The Answer Ministry.** The church where she loves teaching and the Disciples love learning. To God be the Glory for all that is learned and taught.

---

We are the church that read our Bibles to mature.

When we read our Bibles then we know for sure.

So when I go home today I will continue to read the Bible for myself, so that I won't be deceived by anyone else.

Inspired by the Holy Ghost

## DEDICATION

I would first like to dedicate this book to my Lord and Savior Jesus Christ. He is truly my all and all. Without Him I would not have been able to do any of this. If the lessons in this book can win one soul for Christ or bring a backslider back home or motivate the Christians to read and study their Bible more, then my living and writing would not have been in vain. To God truly be the Glory.

To my parents Roosevelt and Corine Gary, To my dear husband Hayward, To all my children whom I love so dearly, Christal Shalon, Tyree Lavelle, Diane Danielle and China Corine, To all my grandchildren who I love even more, Narvell, Taelar, Mya, Arteshia, Alyia and Tyree Jr.

## PASTOR RORIE'S INFO

Overseer L. Rorie, founder and pastor of Prayer Is The Answer Ministry. She was called to preach the gospel in the late 70's. She completed and passed her courses with Aenon Bible College that required her to receive the credentials for her Ordination to preach the Gospel of Jesus Christ. She was Licensed and Ordained into the gospel in July 2000 under the Pentecostal Assembly Of The World (PAW).

For further information or speaking engagements you may e-mail her at ladyrorie@comcast.net or visit the church website at prayeristheanswerministry.com or you may write to her at Prayer is The Answer Ministry, P.O. Box 1051, Bolingbrook Il. 60440.

# LESSON 1

## WHO AND WHAT ARE YOU LISTENING TO?

Adam and Eve dwelled in a paradise called the Garden of Eden. At this particular time there was no sin at all. There were no doctors because there was no sickness. No violence, no hatred, no discord nothing but peace and love. God had given Adam and Eve specific instructions on which trees to eat from and which one that was forbidden.

Well one day Eve was in the garden and she was approached by a serpent. The serpent told Eve that she could eat from the very tree that God told her that should not eat from. She listened, obeyed and she ate the forbidden fruit of that tree. Not only did she eat of the forbidden fruit she also gave to her husband Adam.

Now Eve was truly deceived by the serpent but Adam willingly transgressed. This was the beginning of sin. Sin originated from disobedience through one man. Every since then the world has been in a bad situation with sin running rampant in the earth. It is so important that we obey the voice of God. When we are disobedient and listen and talk to others that have no connection or relationship with God sin is inevitable. Be careful who you are taking advice from. The spirit of the serpent is yet loose today. He is still talking but you don't have to listen you have a choice.

**1. Gen. 3:1**—Now the Serpent was more subtle than any beast of the field which the Lord God had made. And he said unto the woman, Yea, hath God said, Ye shall _____ _____ of every _____ _____ _____ _____?

**2. Gen. 3:2**—And the woman said unto the serpent, we may eat of the _____ of the _____ of the _____.

**3. Gen. 3:3**—But of the fruit of the tree which is in the midst of the _____, God hath said, ye _____ not _____ _____ _____, neither shall ye touch it, _____ _____ _____.

**4. Gen. 3:4**—And the serpent said unto the _____, ye _____ _____ _____ _____.

**5. Gen. 3:5**—For God doth know that in the day ye eat thereof, then your eyes shall _____ _____, and ye shall be as gods, _____ _____ _____ _____.

**6. Gen. 3:6**—And when the woman saw that the tree was good for food, and that it was pleasant to the eyes, and a tree to be desired to make one wise, she took of the _____ thereof, and did eat, and gave also unto her _____ with her; _____ _____ _____ _____.

**7. Gen. 3:7**—And the eyes of them both _____ _____, and they knew that they were naked; and they sewed fig leaves together, and made themselves aprons.

**8. Gen. 3:8**—And they heard the voice of the Lord God walking in the _____ in the _____ _____ _____ _____: and Adam and his wife hid themselves from the presence of the _____ _____ amongst the _____ of the garden.

**9. Gen. 3:9**—And the _____ _____ called unto _____, and said unto him, _____ _____ _____?

**10.  Gen. 3:10**—And he said, I _____ _____ _____ _____ _____ _____, and I was _____, because I was _____; and _____ _____ _____.

**11.  Gen. 3:11**—And he said, _____ _____ _____ _____ _____ _____ _____? Hast thou eaten of the tree, whereof I commanded thee that thou should _____ _____?

**12.  Gen. 3:12**—And the man said, the woman whom thou gave to be with me, she gavest me of the tree, and I _____ _____.

# LESSON 2

## AM I GRIEVING GOD TODAY?

After the disobedience of Adam and Eve this was the beginning of sin. The earth was no longer the perfect paradise that God had intended for it to be. It was frightening to see how all of humanity had forgotten about God. God says that He saw their wickedness and man was doing every sinful and wicked thing imaginable and in these things they did continually. There was only one man on this earth that worshiped and adored God. That man was Noah. A just man and perfect in his generation.

All of mankind on the face of the earth was destroyed because of sin. Because of Noah's faithfulness and obedience, God saved him and his family from the vast flood. God hates sin and judges them who enjoy practicing it. The Bible tells us that the Lord repented for creating man and placing him on earth.

Their disobedience and wickedness broke the heart of God. Even as I read this it grieves my spirit to know that God's heart was broken because of his creation. The same thing that was going on back then is going on today. There is yet disobedience violence and wickedness in the land. We are grieving the heart of God again. Think about it? Do you want God to repent for the day He brought you into creation? Don't we owe God more than heartaches?

**1. Gen. 6:5**—And God saw that the _____ of man was great in the earth, and that every imagination of the thoughts of his heart was only _____ continually.

**2. Gen. 6:6**—And it _____ the _____ that he had made _____ on the _____, and it grieved him at his _____.

**3. Gen. 6:7**—And the lord said, I will destroy man whom I have _____ from the _____ of the earth; both man, and beast, and the creeping thing, and the fowls of the air; for it _____ _____ that I have made _____.

**4. Gen. 6:8**—But _____ found _____ in the _____ _____ _____ _____.

**5. Gen. 6:9**—These are the _____ of Noah: Noah was a just man and perfect in his generations, and Noah walked _____ _____.

**6. Gen. 6:10**—And Noah begat three sons, _____, _____, and _____.

**7. Gen. 6:11**—The earth also was corrupt before God, and the earth was _____ _____ _____.

**8. Gen. 6:12**—And God looked upon the _____, and, behold, it was _____; for all flesh had corrupted his way _____ _____ _____.

**9. Gen. 6:13**—And God said unto _____, The end of all _____ is come before me; for the _____ is filled with violence through them; and, behold, I will _____ them with the earth.

**10.** **Gen.6:14**—Make thee an ark of _____ wood; rooms shall thou make in the _____, and shall pitch it within and without with pitch.

**11.** **Gen. 6:17**—And, behold, I, even I, do bring a flood of waters upon the earth, to _____ _____ _____, wherein is the breath of life, from under _____; and everything that is in the _____ _____ _____.

**12.** **Gen. 6:18**—But with thee will I establish my covenant; and thou shall come into the _____, thou, and thy sons, and thy _____, and thy _____, _____ with thee.

# LESSON 3

## A NEW EARTH

In chapter 7 of Genesis, God told Noah that it was going to rain for forty days and forty nights until he had wiped out the earth. This lesson tells about how God blessed Noah his sons and their wives. God told them to be fruitful and multiply, and replenish the earth. As we know the earth was destroyed because of man's disobedience. God had told Noah in chapter 7 "Go into the Ark with all your family." God said among all the people on the earth—He could see that he (Noah) was most righteous. Now mind you besides Noah's wife, Noah's three sons and their wives, God told Noah to take seven of every kind of animal, male and female on the ark and also take seven of every kind of bird—male and female on the ark. This is the beginning of our new earth.

**1. Gen. 9:1**—And God blessed Noah and his sons, and said unto them, _____ _____, _____ _____, and replenish the earth.

**2. Gen. 9:2**—And the fear of you and the dread of you shall be upon _____ _____ of the earth, and upon every _____ _____ _____ _____, upon all that move upon the earth; and upon all fishes of the sea; into your hand are they delivered.

**3. Gen. 9:3**—Every moving thing that shall be _____ for you; even as the _____ _____ have I given you all things.

**4. Gen. 9:4**—But flesh with the life thereof, which is the blood thereof, shall_____ _____ _____.

**5. Gen. 9:5**—And surely your blood of your lives will I require; at the hand of _____ _____ will I require it, and at the hand of man; at the hand of every man's brother will I require the _____ _____ _____.

**6. Gen. 9:6**—Whoso sheddeth man's blood, by man shall his blood be shed: for in the _____ of _____ made he man.

**7. Gen. 9:7**—And you, be ye fruitful, and multiply; bring forth abundantly in the _____, and _____ therein.

**8. Gen. 9:8**—And God _____ unto Noah, and to his sons with him saying,

**9. Gen. 9:9**—And I, behold, I establish my covenant with you, and with _____ _____ after _____.

# LESSON 4

## ABRAHAM A MAN OF FAITH

Abraham obeyed God when He instructed him to leave his home and go to a foreign land. Abraham went without knowing where he was going. He went by faith. The supreme test of Abraham's faith came when God commanded him to sacrifice Isaac. Abraham obeyed faithfully, trusting God with his promised son. Well, just as the knife was about to fall, the angel of the Lord stopped Abraham and provided a ram for him to sacrifice in place of his son Isaac. Abraham was offering Isaac as a sacrifice when being tried of God (Heb. 11:17). The offering of his son was by faith and obedience.

The hallmark of Abraham's life was that he trusted and had faith in God. The Lord God considered him righteous because of his faith. Abraham's righteousness was not because he never sinned because on several occasions he failed to make the right decisions.

Today we don't have to give our children or animals in sacrifices. Jesus gave his life so that he would be the perfect sacrifice for all of mankind. Think about the faith that Abraham had. Are we willing to go anywhere or do anything without questioning God? Are you prepared to trust God in faith and do what he has commissioned you to do? Are you ready to say yes to His will for your life?

**1. Gen. 12:1**—Now the Lord had said unto Abram, Get thee out of thy country, and from thy kindred, and from thy father's house, unto a _____ that I will shew thee:

**2. Gen. 12:2**—And I will make thee a _____ nation, and I will _____ _____, and make thy name great; and thou shalt be a _____:

**3. Gen. 12:3**—And I will _____ them that bless thee, and _____ him that _____ thee: and in thee shall all _____ of the earth be blessed.

**4. Gen. 12:4**—So _____ departed, as the Lord had spoken unto him; and _____ went with him: and Abram was _____ and _____ years old when he departed out if Haran.

**5. Gen. 12:5**—And Abram took _____ his wife, and Lot his _____ _____, and all their substance that they had gathered, and the souls that they had gotten in Haran; and they went forth to go into the land of Canaan; and into the land of Canaan they came.

**6. Gen. 12:6**—And _____ passed through the land unto the place of Sichem unto the plain of _____. And the _____ was then in the land.

**7. Gen. 12:7**—And the Lord appeared unto Abram, and said, unto thy _____ will I give this _____; and there builded he an altar unto the _____, who appeared unto him.

**8. Gen. 17:1**—And when _____ was ninety years old and _____, the Lord appeared to Abram, and said unto him, _____ _____ _____ _____ _____; walk before me, and be thou perfect.

**9. Gen. 17:2**—And I will make _____ _____ between me and thee, and will _____ thee exceedingly.

**10.  Gen. 17:4**—As for me, behold, my _____ is with thee, and thou shalt be a _____ _____ _____ _____.

**11.   11. Gen. 17:5**—Neither shall thy _____ any more be _____ _____, but thy name shall be _____; for a _____ of many nations have I _____ _____.

## LESSON 5

### SARAH A MOTHER OF NATIONS

This is a story about a woman by the name of Sarai. Sarai was the wife of Abram (Abraham). Sarai was among the women in the Bible who were barren but she miraculously bore a son. The Lord knew how much Sarai wanted to give her husband a son. Sarai wanted to give her husband a son so badly that out of love she asked her husband to take her handmaiden Hagar into his bed.

God told Abraham that he was going to bless Sarai and give her a son. God said that He was going to bless her and she would be the mother of nations and Kings of people shall come from her. Everything that God was promising Sarai and her husband they found a bit amusing because of Sarai's age. We must believe the promises of God and not sway at them. If God said it, then, it is so. All we have to do is stay focused and don't give up on the word that God has spoken.

Sarai birthed her first son just like God said at the age of ninety. If God said it then we must believe it. After the birth of their son Isaac God changed her name from Sarai to Sarah. Sarah means princess. Who would have thought that the ninety year old woman would give birth? Because the promises don't always come when we think it should that does not mean that it is not going to. Remember delay does not mean denied.

**1. Gen. 17:15**—And God said unto Abraham, As for Sarai thy wife, thou shalt not call her _____ _____, but _____ shall her _____ _____.

**2. Gen. 17:16**—And I will bless her, and give thee a son also of her; yea, _____ _____ _____ _____, and she shall be a _____ _____ _____; kings of people shall be of her.

**3. Gen. 16:1**—Now Sarai Abram's wife bare him no children: and she had an handmaid, an _____, whose name was _____.

**4. Gen.16:2**—And Sarai said unto Abram, Behold now, the Lord hath _____ me from _____: I pray thee go in unto my _____; it may be that I may obtain children by her. And Abram hearkened to the voice of Sarai.

**5. Gen. 16:4**—And he went into _____, and she _____: and when she saw that she had conceived, her mistress was _____ in her eyes.

**6. Gen. 16:15**—And _____ bare _____ a son: and Abram called his son's name, which _____ bare, _____.

**7. Gen 16:16**—And Abram was _____ and six years old, when _____ _____ Ishmael to _____.

**8. Gen. 17:17**—Then Abraham fell upon his face, and laughed, and said in his heart, Shall a child be born unto him that is an _____ _____ _____? And shall Sarah, that is ninety years old, bear?

**9. Gen. 17:21**—But my _____ will I establish with _____, which _____ shall bear unto thee at this _____ _____ in the next year.

**10.** **Gen. 21:1**—And the Lord visited _____ as he had said, and the Lord did unto Sarah as he had spoken.

**11.** **Gen. 21:2**—For Sarah _____ and bare Abraham a _____ _____ _____ _____ _____, at the set time of which God had spoken to him.

**12.** **Gen. 21:3**—And Abraham called the name of his son that was born unto him, whom _____ bare to him, Isaac.

# LESSON 6

## WHAT DID GOD SAY DO?

It has been 37 years since Israel's first spy mission into the Promised Land and 40 years since the exit from Egypt. The Bible is virtually silent for about those 37 years of aimless wandering. The generation which Moses had delivered out of Egypt had mostly died off and there's a new generation that would soon be ready to enter the Promise Land.

As you read into the story you will observe that the people are complaining the more. Complaining that they have no water, they have no food, how much further, I'm tired. The people have been complaining and murmuring since they left Egypt and now their children are picking up where they left off with the complaining.

God wants to show the people his power. God asks Moses and Aaron to gather all the people together at a particular site in front of this rock. He gives Moses instructions so that the people can witness the power of God and build up their faith. Moses was so frustrated and angry with the people because of their lack of trust and complaining that he disobeyed God.

We must not ever allow people to have us so annoyed that we disobey God. The disobedience of Moses caused him not to be able to enter the Promise Land. Don't allow people to make you miss your promise.

1. **Num.20:2**—And there was _____ _____ for the _____: and they gathered themselves together against Moses and against _____.

2. **Num. 20:3**—And the people chode with Moses, and spake, saying, Would God that we had died when our brethren _____ before _____ _____!

3. **Num. 20:7**—And the _____ _____ unto Moses, _____,

4. **Num. 20:8**—Take the _____, and _____ thou the _____ _____ together, thou, and Aaron thy brother, and _____ ye unto the _____ before their eyes; and it shall give forth his _____, and thou shalt bring forth to them _____ out of _____ _____: so thou shalt give the congregation and their beasts drink.

5. **Num. 20:9**—And _____ took the _____ from before the Lord, as he _____ _____.

6. **Num.20:10**—And _____ and _____ gathered the congregation together before the _____ and he said unto them, Hear now, ye _____; must we fetch you _____ _____ _____ _____ _____?

7. **Num. 20:11**—And Moses lifted up his hand and with his rod he _____ the _____ _____: and the _____ came _____ _____, and the congregation _____, and their beasts also.

8. **Num. 20:12**—And the Lord spake unto _____ and _____, Because ye believed me not, to sanctify me in the eyes of the _____ _____ _____, therefore ye shall not bring this congregation into the land which I have given them.

**9. Deut. 1:37**—Also the _____ _____ _____ with me for your sakes, saying, Thou also shalt not go in thither.

**10.  Deut. 34:4**—And the Lord said unto him, This is the land which I _____ unto _____, unto Isaac, and unto _____, saying, I will give it unto thy seed: I have caused thee to see it with thine eyes, but thou shalt _____ _____ _____ _____.

**11.  Deut. 34:5**—So Moses the _____ of the Lord died there in the land of _____, according to the word of the Lord.

# LESSON 7

## THE PRECIOUS LAMB OF GOD

The Passover is an eight day holiday in observance commemorating the freedom and exodus (exit) of the Israelite (Jewish Slaves) from Egypt during the reign of the Pharaoh. The name Passover came about when Pharaoh refused to let the Israelites go. God was going to send a plague that was going to kill all of the first born (Ex. 12:29). To show that you were on the Lord side the people of God had to take the blood of a lamb and spread it in the door post of their homes.

This lamb had to be without spot or blemish. This lamb had to be without any defects at all. When God saw the blood of the lamb over the door post of the house, this would be the house that He would Passover and death would not serve notice to their first born.

In the days of the Old Testament the sacrifice of the blood of the lamb was chosen to save them from destruction. Today the only lamb that can save us is Jesus. John 1:29 says "The next day John seeth Jesus coming unto him, and saith, Behold the Lamb of God, which taketh away the sin of the world." We don't have to use the blood of animals for our atonement. Our perfect sacrifice was the blood of Jesus, The Precious Lamb of God.

**1. Ex. 12:1**—And The Lord spake unto Moses and Aaron in the land of _____, saying,

**2. Ex. 12:2**—This month shall be unto you the beginning of months: it shall be the _____ _____ of the year to you.

**3. Ex. 12:3**—Speak ye unto all the congregation of Israel, saying, In the _____ _____ of this month they shall take to them every man a _____, according to the house of their fathers, a _____ for an _____:

**4. Ex. 12:4**—And if the _____ be too little for the _____, let him and his _____ next unto his house take it according to the _____ of the _____; every man according to his eating shall make your _____ for the _____.

**5. Ex. 12:5**—Your lamb shall be _____ _____, a _____ of the first year: ye shall take it out from the _____, or from the _____:

**6. Ex. 12:6**—And ye shall keep it up until the fourteenth day of the same month: and the whole assembly of the congregation of _____ _____ _____ it in the evening.

## LESSON 8

### LORD DELIVER ME

You are about to read and learn about one of the most talked about miracles of all times. God sent Moses to Pharaoh to tell him to let the children of Israel go. They had been in bondage a little over 400 years and their time for deliverance had come. Some of you have been in bondage to the things and the ways of this world. I pray when you study this lesson that you have the faith to know that the same God that delivered the children of Israel can also deliver you. Pharaoh allowed them to leave, only to renege on his word and go after them.

The children of Israel looked back only to see that Pharaoh's army was on their trail. We spend too much time looking back. Once God has freed us from something or someone we need to look forward. We have the victory and our promise is in front of us. We lose time when we look back and remembering when.

God rolled up the sea so that the Israelites could cross to the other side. When they couldn't see their way God made a way out of no way. We all go through things from time to time and it looks like there is no way out but if we would just trust God he will roll back the sea so that you can get to the other side.

**1. Ex. 14:15**—And the Lord said unto Moses, Wherefore criest thou unto me? Speak unto the _____ _____ _____, that they go forward:

**2. Ex. 14:16**—But lift thou up thy rod, and stretch out thine hand over the sea, and divide it: and the children of Israel shall go on _____ _____ through the midst of the sea.

**3. Ex. 14:17**—And I, behold, I, will harden the hearts of the Egyptians, and they shall follow them: and I will get me honour upon Pharaoh, and upon all his host, upon his chariots, and upon _____ _____.

**4. Ex. 14:18**—And the _____ shall know that I am the _____, when I have gotten me honour upon Pharaoh, _____ _____ _____, and upon his horsemen.

**5. Ex. 14:19**—And the _____ _____ _____, which went before _____ _____ _____ _____, removed and went behind them; and the pillar of the cloud went from before their face, and stood behind them:

**6. Ex. 14:20**—And it came between the _____ _____ _____ _____ and the camp of Israel; and it was a _____ and _____ to them, but it gave light by night to these: so that the one came not near the other all the night.

**7. Ex. 14:21**—And Moses stretched out his hand over the sea; and the _____ caused the _____ to go back by a strong _____ _____ all that night, and made the _____ _____ _____, and the waters were divided.

**8. Ex. 14:22**—And the _____ _____ _____ went into the midst of the _____ upon the dry ground: and the _____ were a _____ unto them on their right hand, and on their left.

**9. Ex. 14:23**—And the _____ _____, and went in after them to the midst of the _____, even all Pharaoh's horses, his chariots, and his horsemen.

**10.    Ex. 14:24**—And it came to pass, that in the morning watch the Lord looked unto the host of the _____ through the pillar of _____ and of the _____, and troubled the _____ _____ the Egyptians.

**11.    Ex. 14:25**—And took off their chariot wheels, that they drave them heavily: so that the _____ said, Let us flee from the face of _____; for the Lord fighteth for them _____ _____ _____.

**12.    Ex. 14:30**—Thus the _____ _____ Israel that day out of the hand of the _____; and _____ saw the _____ _____ upon the sea shore.

# LESSON 9

## What's Your Excuse?

Moses was a man called and chosen by God. God wanted Moses to go to the Pharaoh with a message. This should have been an honor and a privilege to be commissioned by God. This was not Mosses' first encounter with the Lord so he was no stranger to Him. Instead of Moses preparing to do what God had asked of him, he thought of a reason why he shouldn't do it.

Moses was challenged in his speaking. Moses felt like if he went to Pharaoh that he may laugh at him or not take him serious. Moses could have been embarrassed to speak publicly because of his challenge or he could have been intimidated to speak to someone such as the Pharaoh. Moses then asked God to send his brother Aaron. Moses felt like his brother was more articulate than he was.

We should never feel as though God won't use us because of our physical challenges. Man may not use you because of your limitations but in God there are no limits. There are no physical challenges. God is not looking at the physical ability of the man but at the heart and the spirit of the man. Don't limit yourself to what man may say about you in your physical challenge. What is God saying? Using your challenge as a way not to obey God is willingly transgressing against God. If we would just say yes, be obedient and trust God. He will meet you right where you are even in our challenges, we are over comers!

---

**1. Ex. 4:10**—And Moses said unto the Lord, O my Lord, I am not _____, neither heretofore, nor since thou hast spoken unto thy servant: but _____ _____ _____ _____ _____, and of a _____ _____.

**2. Ex. 4:11**—And the lord said unto him, Who hath made man's mouth? Or who maketh the _____, or _____, or the seeing, or the blind? _____ _____ _____ _____ _____?

**3. Ex. 4:12**—Now therefore go, and I will be with _____ _____, and _____ thee _____ thou _____ _____.

**4. Ex. 4:13**—And he said, _____ _____ _____, send, _____ _____ _____, by the hand of him whom thou wilt send.

**5. Ex. 4:14**—And the anger of the Lord was kindled against Moses, and he said, Is not Aaron the Levite the brother? I know that he can _____ _____. And also, behold, he cometh forth to meet thee: and when he seeth thee, he will be glad _____ _____ _____.

**6. Ex. 4:15**—And thou shalt speak unto him, and put words in his _____: and I will be with thy _____, and with _____ _____, and will _____ you what ye shall do.

**7. Ex. 4:16**—And he shall be thy spokesman unto the people: and he shall be, even he shall be to thee instead of a _____, and thou shalt be to him instead of God.

**8. Ex. 4:27**—And the Lord said to _____, Go into the _____ to _____ _____. And he went, and met him in the mount of God, and kissed him.

**9. Ex. 4:28**—And _____ _____ _____ all the _____ of the _____ who had sent him, and all the signs which he had commanded him.

**10. Ex. 4:29**—And Moses and Aaron went and gathered together all the _____ of the _____ of _____:

# LESSON 10

## THE PROPHECY AND THE PROMISE

After the fall of Adam and Eve their lives could never be the same again. Their transgression had stained the conscience of all mankind to come. They had sinned against God and this was something that each generation after them had to bear the burden of. In the single most important test of their lives they had failed. But God made a covenant with Adam and Eve and with all that was to come after them.

The promise was that a Messiah would redeem them from their sins. That promise was fulfilled in the coming of Jesus Christ. The prophet Isaiah foretold of this promise back in the Old Testament—way before Jesus was born. After four hundred years of prophetic silence the birth of the Messiah came to past.

After the silence there came a man by the name of John the Baptist who would be a voice in the wilderness that would cry, "Prepare ye the way of the Lord, make straight in the desert a highway for our God." As John the Baptist comes, the work of preparation continues. His was a message and a baptism of repentance. The Kingdom of heaven was at hand, even now upon the earth today. Jesus wants us to preach Kingdom and not denomination. Preach Jesus until He returns.

**1. Isaiah 40:3**—The voice of him that crieth in the wilderness, Prepare ye the _____ _____ _____ _____, make straight in the desert a highway for our God.

**2. Isaiah 40:4**—Every valley shall be exalted, and every mountain and hill shall be made low: and the crooked shall be made straight, and the _____ _____ _____:

**3. Isaiah 40:5**—And the glory of the Lord shall be revealed, and all flesh shall see it together: for the mouth of the Lord _____ _____.

**4. John 1:15**—John bare witness of him, and cried, saying, This was he of whom I spake, He that _____ after me is preferred _____ _____: for he was before me.

**5. John 1:16**—And of his _____ have all we received, and _____ _____ _____.

**6. John 1:17**—For the law was given by Moses, but grace and _____ _____ _____ _____ _____.

**7. John 1:18**—No man hath seen _____ at any time; the only _____ _____, which is in the bosom of the _____, he hath declared him.

**8. John 1:19**—And this is the record of John, when the Jews sent priests and Levites from Jerusalem to ask him, _____ _____ _____?

**9. John 1:20**—And _____ _____, and denied not; but _____, I am not _____ _____.

10. **John 1:21**—And they asked him, What then? Art thou Elias And he saith, _____ _____ _____. Art thou that _____? And he answered, No.

11. **John 1:22**—Then said they unto him, _____ _____ _____? That we may give an answer to them that sent us. _____ _____ thou of thyself?

12. **John 1:23**—He said, _____ _____ _____ _____ of one crying in the wilderness, Make straight the way of the Lord, as said the prophet Esaias.

# LESSON 11

## PROPITIATION

Propitiation is the atoning death of Jesus on the cross, through which He paid the penalty demanded by God for the sins of the people, thus setting them free from sin and death. The word means "appeasement." Thus, propitiation expresses the idea that Jesus died on the cross to pay the price for sin that a holy God demanded. Propitiation refers to the removal of that which is displeasing in one party so that the two can be brought together. It is very similar to reconciliation indicating bringing two parties together. Although Jesus never sinned, knew no sin, and was free of sin, He took all our sins upon Himself and redeemed us from the penalty of death.

---

1. **1ˢᵗ John 2:2**—And he is the _____ for our sins: and not for ours only, but also for the _____ of the _____ _____.

2. **1ˢᵗ John 4:10**—Herein is love, not that we _____ _____, but that He _____ _____, and sent his Son to be the _____ for _____ _____.

3. **Rom. 3:25**—Whom God hath set forth to be a _____ through _____ in his _____, to declare his righteousness for the remission of sins that are past, through the forbearance of God;

# LESSON 12

## ATONEMENT

In the Bible atonement is associated with the sins of man. Atonement means a payment or offering to remove or forgive sin. God commanded Israel to set aside one day each year, the tenth day of the seventh month, which he called the Day of Atonement. On the Day of Atonement an innocent animal be sacrificed whose blood was brought in to make atonement for the people of God.

Sin is the cause of the estrangement between God and His people and therefore the purpose of atonement is to correct or overcome the consequences of sin. From the time of Adam to the death of Jesus Christ, true believers were instructed to offer make sacrifice's unto the Lord.

When Jesus died, He gave his own life as the perfect sacrifice for the atonement of His people. God sending His own Son in the likeness of sinful flesh, and for sin, condemned sin in the flesh, was the only one capable of making atonement for mankind.

The word atonement is used more in the Old Testament than the New Testament. The word atonement is only used once in the New Testament and there it is translated as Reconciliation in the revised King James Bible.

**1. Lev. 23:26**—And the Lord spake unto ＿＿＿＿＿＿, saying,

**2. Lev. 23:27**—Also on this ＿＿＿＿＿ ＿＿＿＿＿ of the ＿＿＿＿＿ ＿＿＿＿＿ there shall be a day of atonement: it shall be an ＿＿＿＿＿ convocation unto you; and ye shall afflict your souls, and offer an offering made by ＿＿＿＿＿ ＿＿＿＿＿ ＿＿＿＿＿ Lord.

**3. Lev. 23:28**—And ye shall do no work in that same day: for it is a ＿＿＿＿＿ ＿＿＿＿＿ ＿＿＿＿＿, to make an atonement for you before the Lord your God.

**4. He. 9:22**—And almost all things are by the law purged with blood; and without ＿＿＿＿＿ ＿＿＿＿＿ ＿＿＿＿＿ is no ＿＿＿＿＿.

**5. He. 10:1**—FOR THE law having a shadow of good things to come, and not the very image of the things, can never with those sacrifices which they offered ＿＿＿＿＿ by year continually make the ＿＿＿＿＿ thereunto perfect.

**6. He. 10:2**—For then would they not have ceased to be offered? Because that the worshippers once purged should have had no more ＿＿＿＿＿ of ＿＿＿＿＿.

**7. He. 10:3**—But in those ＿＿＿＿＿ there is a remembrance again made of ＿＿＿＿＿ every ＿＿＿＿＿.

**8. He. 10:4**—For it is not ＿＿＿＿＿ that the blood of bulls and of ＿＿＿＿＿ should take away sins.

**9. He. 10:5**—Wherefore when he cometh into the world, he saith, ＿＿＿＿＿ ＿＿＿＿＿ ＿＿＿＿＿ thou wouldest not, but a ＿＿＿＿＿ hast thou prepared me:

**10. He. 10:6**—In burnt offerings and ＿＿＿＿＿ for sin thou hast had no pleasure.

**11.** **He. 10:9**—Then said he, Lo, I come to do thy will, O God. He taketh away the first, that he may _____ the second.

**12.** **He. 10:10**—By the which will we are _____ through the offering of the _____ of Jesus Christ once for all.

**13.** **Rom. 5:11**—And not only so, but we also joy in God through our _____ _____ _____, by whom we have now received the atonement.

# LESSON 13

## What Are We Really Watching?

We hear so much about the world coming to an end. I have been hearing about different dates and times that the world should be ending since I was a little girl. Every time I heard these rumors I would always be frightened by what I was hearing. After I was older and came into the knowledge of Jesus, I began to build a relationship with Him as my personal Savior. In doing this I got a better understanding from the Bible and not man.

Now that I abide in Christ I know without a shadow of a doubt that no man knows when Jesus will return. This lesson tells us that no man knows the day nor the hour when Jesus shall return not even the angels in heaven shall know. No one knows that time except the Father in heaven. Since we don't know the arrival date of Christ we should always be prepared.

We should treat each day as if it's our last. We should love everyone with the Love of Jesus. We should treat everyone with respect and dignity. We should never let the sun go down on our anger. The night we do that could be the return of the Lord. Let's not take it for granted that because we are going to sleep healthy that we have to wake up the same. Are you really watching for the sky to open and praying to Jesus or are you watching too much television and gossiping?

**1. Matt. 24:36**—But of that day and hour knoweth no man, no, not the _____ _____ _____, but my Father only.

**2. Matt. 24:37**—But as the days of Noe were, so shall also the coming of the Son _____ _____ _____.

**3. Matt. 24:38**—For as in the days that were before the flood they were _____ _____ _____, marrying and giving in marriage, until the day that Noe entered into the ark,

**4. Matt. 24:39**—And knew not until the _____ came, and took them all away; so shall also the coming of the Son of _____ _____.

**5. Matt. 24:40**—Then shall two be in the field; the one shall be taken, _____ _____ _____ _____.

**6. Matt. 24:41**—Two women shall be grinding at the mill; the one _____ _____ _____, and the other left.

**7. Matt. 24:42**—Watch therefore: for ye know not what hour your _____ _____ _____.

**8. Matt. 24:43**—But know this, that if the goodman of the house had known in what watch the thief would come, he would have _____, and would not have suffered his house _____ _____ _____ _____.

# LESSON 14

## SPIRITUAL ADOPTION

Adoption is the act of voluntarily accepting responsibility of a child. Adoption is the term the apostle Paul uses to describe the act of the Holy Spirit whereby the new believer becomes a member of God's Family, with all rights and privileges. It is the Holy Spirit who is called the Spirit of adoption who performs the act of placing the converted sinner into the family of God. "For you have not received a spirit of slavery leading to bondage again, but you have received a spirit of adoption as sons by whom we cry out, Abba Father!

Through spiritual adoption, believers are made to be sons of God, heirs with Abraham, and partakers of the promises of the covenant God made with the patriarch. And since believers are adopted, they are no longer slaves but sons, and if sons, then heirs of God through Christ (Gal. 4:7). Because Jesus Christ paid the ultimate price for our redemption, nothing stands in the way of a just God regenerating a sinner and placing him as His child in His family. The Holy Spirit as the Spirit of adoption also places a converted sinner in a legal standing in God's family. Don't you want to be in the family of God? Join us.

**1. Rom. 8:15**—For ye have not received the _____ of _____ again to fear; but ye have received the Spirit of _____, whereby we cry, Abba, Father.

**2. Rom. 8:16-17**—The _____ itself beareth witness with our _____, that we are the _____ of _____: And if _____, then _____; heirs of God, and joint _____ with _____; If so be that we may suffer with Him, that we may be also _____ together.

**3. Rom. 8:23**—And not only they, but ourselves also, which have the _____ of the _____, even we ourselves groan within ourselves, waiting for the _____, to wit, the _____ of our body.

**4. Rom. 9:4**—Who are Israelites; to whom pertaineth the _____, and the _____, and the covenants and the giving of the _____, and the service of _____., and the _____;

**5. Gal. 4:5**—To _____ them that were under the _____, that we might receive the _____ of _____.

# LESSON 15

## GOD'S SALVATION PLAN

Salvation is deliverance from the power of sin. The salvation that comes through Christ may be described in three tenses: past, present, and future. The Bible says that if we believe on the Lord Jesus Christ, that we shalt be saved (Acts 16:31). But we are also in the process of being saved from the power of sin (Rom. 8:13; Phil. 2:12). Finally, we shall be saved from the very presence of sin (Rom. 13:11; Titus 2:12-13). The Bible says in Eph. 2:8 "For by grace are ye saved through faith; and that not of yourselves: It is the gift of God".

The need for salvation goes back to the removal of Adam and Eve from the Garden of Eden (Gen. 3). Salvation means the act of saving someone from the act of sin that leads to destruction and failure. Salvation is deliverance from sin through Jesus Christ our Lord. The Bible says that we have all sinned and come short of the glory of God.

We needed a Savior to deliver us from sin and evil. Our Savior is just that. He is the only one who can save us. Jesus is standing at the door of all of our hearts. He is waiting for us to invite Him in. The Bible tells us "She shall bring forth a son, and thou shalt call his name JESUS: for he shall save his people from their sins" (Matt.1:21).

Until we come into the fold and accept Jesus Christ as our personal Savior we will always be lost. John 3:17 says that "For God sent not his Son into the world to condemn the world; but that the world through him might be saved."

---

**1. Rom. 10:9**—That if thou _____ _____ with thy mouth the _____ _____, and shalt _____ in thine _____ that _____ hath raised him from the _____ thou shalt be _____

**2. Acts 4:12**—Neither is there _____ in any other: for there is none other name under heaven given among men, whereby we _____ _____ _____.

**3. Acts 15:11**—But we believe that through the grace of the Lord Jesus Christ _____ _____ _____ _____, even as they.

**4. Eph. 2:8**—For by _____ are ye _____ through faith; and that not of _____: it is the gift of God:

**5. Rom. 6:23**—For the _____ of _____ is _____; but the _____ of God is eternal life through _____ _____ _____ _____

**6. Rom. 3:23**—For _____ _____ _____ and come short of the _____ of _____;

**7. John 3:3**—Jesus answered and said unto him, Verily, verily, I say unto thee, Except a man be _____ _____ he cannot see the kingdom of God.

**8. John 3:5**—Jesus answered and said unto him, Verily, verily, I say unto thee, Except a man be _____ _____ _____ and of and of the _____, he _____ enter into the kingdom of God.

**9. John 3:6**—That which is _____ of the _____ is _____; and that which is _____ of the _____ is _____.

**10. Rom. 10:10**—For with the _____ man believeth unto righteousness; and with the _____ confession is made unto _____.

**11. Luke 13:5**—I tell you, Nay: but, except ye repent, ye shall all likewise _____.

**12. Rom. 5:8**—But God commendeth his love toward us, in that, while we were yet sinners, _____ died for us.

# LESSON 16

## CHRIST THE TRUE VINE

This chapter starts off by saying that Jesus is the True Vine and his father (God) is the husbandman. Jesus is using the analogy where He is a vine and His father was called the Vine Dresser. The analogy of the vine can help us to understand how we should be connected to Jesus just as He is connected to His Father, the Vine Dresser. Jesus is the vine and not just any old vine but He is the True Vine and we are the branches. We should bear the fruit of the vine that we come from. It's no way that we can be the branches of an apple tree but yet we are producing pears.

When we say that we are Christians this is saying pertaining to Christ. This is saying that we want to be like Him. We are saying that He abides in us as we abide in Him. Since God is the Father of us all then we should bear the characteristics of our Heavenly Father. Our Heavenly Father bears the fruit of love, joy, peace, longsuffering, gentleness, goodness, faith, meekness, and temperance. As branches of the True Vine we should bear the fruit of the spirit which is the fruit of Jesus Christ as He bears the fruit of the Father. Now, if you are cussing, lying, cheating, and fornicating just to name a few then your fruit are fowl. Whatever you have on your vine that is what you are going to produce. Examine your fruit.

**1. John 15:1**—I am the _____ _____, and my Father is the husbandman.

**2. John 15:2**—Every branch in me that beareth not fruit he taketh away: and every branch that beareth fruit, he purgeth it, that it may _____ _____ _____ _____.

**3. John 15:3**—Now ye are clean through the _____ which _____ _____ _____ unto you.

**4. John 15:4**—Abide in me, and I in you. As the branch cannot _____ _____ _____ _____, except it abide in the vine; no more can ye, except ye abide in me.

**5. John 15:5**—I am the vine, _____ _____ _____ _____: He that abideth in me, and I in Him, the same bringeth forth much fruit: for without me ye can do nothing.

**6. John 15:6**—If a man abide not in me, he is cast forth as a _____, _____ _____ _____; and men gather them, and cast them into the fire, and they are burned.

**7. John 15:7**—If ye abide in me, and my words abide in you, ye shall ask what ye will, _____ _____ _____ _____ _____ _____ _____.

**8. John 15:8**—Herein is my _____ glorified, that ye bear _____ _____; so shall ye be my disciples.

**9. John 15:9**—As the Father hath loved me, so have _____ _____ _____: continue ye in my love.

# LESSON 17

## CHRIST THE DIVINE TEACHER

This lesson is about a man by the name of Nicodemus who was the ruler of the Jews in his time. Nicodemus was a knowledgeable, a scholar and an intellect. Nicodemus would go to Jesus by night for Jesus to teach him. I'm assuming that Nicodemus went by night because he didn't want anyone to see him going to Jesus for his knowledge. Nicodemus would have been embarrassed if anyone would have found out that he was getting his knowledge from the son of a carpenter. After all he was the one who was the scholar and the ruler.

Nicodemus had to respect Jesus for who he was. He knew that Jesus was sent by God. Nicodemus even said in the scriptures "Rabbi, we know that thou art a teacher come from God; for no man can do these miracles that thou doest, except God be with him." Jesus is the teacher of all teachers. We must allow Jesus to teach and instruct us even today. When we are in school we are promoted from one grade to the next. It is pretty much the same in God. We will go from level to level in Him. There will be trials and tribulations in our lives. Depending on how we handle the trial whether or not we pass our test. If we respond correctly to a negative situation then we are passed on to the next level.

_____

**1. John 3:1**—There was a man of the Pharisees, named Nicodemus, _____ _____ _____ _____ _____:

**2. John 3:2**—The same came to Jesus by night, and said unto him, Rabbi; we know that thou art a _____ _____ _____ _____: for no man can do these miracles that thou doest, except God be with him.

**3. John 3:3**—Jesus answered and said unto him, Verily, verily, I say unto thee, Except a man be born again, he cannot see the _____ _____ _____.

**4. John 3:4**—Nicodemus saith unto him, how can a man be born when he is old? Can he enter the second time into his _____ _____, _____ _____ _____?

**5. John 3:5**—Jesus answered, Verily, verily, I say unto thee, _____ _____ _____ _____ _____ _____ _____ and of the Spirit, he cannot enter into the kingdom of God.

**6. John 3:6**—That which is born of flesh is flesh; and that which is _____ _____ _____ _____ _____ _____.

# LESSON 18

## DEFILE NOT THE TEMPLE OF GOD

This lesson deals with how we should not defile our bodies. The word of God says that our bodies are the temple of the Holy Ghost. God wants to abide in you and you in Him. We must guard our ear gate, our eye gate and the words that we speak. As being men and women of God we are not to watch, listen and speak things that are of the world.

The scripture says in Romans 12:1-2 that our bodies should be acceptable unto God. Meaning we should not abuse our body or our mind. The Bible also says that we should not be conformed to this world (cigarettes, alcohol, pre-marital sex and drugs,) but be ye transformed by the renewing of your mind. The things we used to do we don't do anymore. We have sanctified our lives and now we are living for Jesus Christ. Additionally, it is not the will of God that we mark our bodies with carvings or engravings of living or deceased relatives.

The body is not meant to be the billboard to advertise with tattooed ink. Your body is for the use of and for the glory of God (Lev. 19:28). You may say "well I didn't know, so now what? Does Jesus hate me?" No, Jesus loves you. From this day forward you are not to mark anymore carvings in your body. As of this day you cannot say that you didn't know. Before we came to Christ we all did things that we shouldn't have done but once we accepted Him we were made new creatures in Jesus Christ our Lord and the things we used to do we no longer do and the places we used to go we no longer go and the words we used to say we no longer say.

**1. 1ˢᵗ Peter 4:3**—For the time past of our life may suffice us to have wrought the will of the Gentiles, when we walked in lasciviousness, lusts, excess of _____, revellings, banqueting, and abominable idolatries:

**2. 1ˢᵗ Peter 4:4**—wherein they think it strange that ye run not with them to the same excess of riot, speaking evil of _____:

**3. 1ˢᵗ Cor. 6:11**—And such were some of you: but ye are washed, but ye are sanctified, but ye are justified in the _____ _____ _____ _____ _____, and by the Spirit of our God.

**4. 1ˢᵗ Cor. 6:12**—All things are lawful unto me, **but all things are not expedient:** all things are lawful for me, but I will not be brought _____ _____ _____ _____ _____.

**5. 1ˢᵗ Cor. 8:12**—But when ye sin so against the brethren, and wound their weak conscience,_____ _____ _____ _____.

**6. 1ˢᵗ Cor. 8:13**—Wherefore, if meat make my brother to offend, I will eat no flesh while the world standeth, lest I make my _____ _____ _____.

**7. Prov. 20:1**—Wine is a mocker, strong drink is raging: and whosoever is deceived thereby _____ _____ _____.

**8. Prov. 3:13**—Happy is the man that findeth wisdom, and the man that _____ _____.

**9. Prov. 4:7**—Wisdom is the principal thing; therefore get wisdom: and with all thy getting get _____.

**10. Prov.9:10**—The fear of the Lord is the beginning of wisdom: and the knowledge of the holy is _____.

11.   **Eph. 5:17**—Wherefore be ye not unwise, but understanding what the _____ _____ _____ _____ _____.

12.   **Eph. 5:18**—And be not _____ _____ _____, wherein is excess; but be filled with the Spirit.

13.   **1ˢᵗ Cor. 3:17**—If any man defile the temple of God, him shall God destroy; for the temple of God is holy, _____ _____ _____ _____.

14.   **Isa. 28:7**—But they also have erred through wine, and through strong drink are out of the way; the priest and the Prophet have erred through strong drink, they are swallowed up of wine, they are out of the way through strong drink; they err in vision, they stumble in _____.

15.   **Lev. 19:28**—Ye shall not make any _____ _____ _____ _____ for the **dead**, nor print any marks upon you: I am the Lord.

# LESSON 19

## Do Not Be Entangled With This World

We live in this world but we are not to be partakers of what this world has to offer. This world is corrupt with sin and evil. We need to be careful that we don't get entangled with the ways of sin, evil, man's traditions and religion. We must know how to live in this world without becoming a part of the world's behaviors and traditions while also being oh so careful of the company that we keep.

1. **Rom. 12:1**—I beseech you therefore, brethren, by the mercies of _____, that ye _____ your bodies a _____ Sacrifice, _____, acceptable unto God, which is your _____ _____.

2. **Rom. 12:2**—And be _____ _____ to this world: but be ye _____ by the _____ of your _____, that ye may prove what is that _____, and acceptable, and _____, will of _____.

3. **2nd Cor. 6:14**—Be ye not _____' _____ together with _____: for what _____ hath _____ with un-righteousness? And what communion hath _____ with _____?

4. **2nd Cor. 6:15**—And what concord hath _____ with Belial? Or what part hath he that _____ with an _____?

**5. 2ⁿᵈ Cor. 6:16**—And what agreement hath the temple of God with _____? For ye are the _____ of the living _____; as God hath said, I will dwell in them; and walk in them; and I will be their _____, and they shall be my people.

**6. 2ⁿᵈ Cor. 6:17**—Wherefore come out from among them, and be ye _____, saith the _____, and touch not the _____ _____; and I will receive you,

**7. 2ⁿᵈ Cor. 6:18**—And will be a Father unto you, and ye shall be my _____ and _____, saith the Lord Almighty.

**8. 2ⁿᵈ Cor. 7:1**—Having therefore these _____, dearly _____, let us cleanse ourselves from all _____ of the _____ and _____, perfecting _____ in the _____ of God.

**9. 1ˢᵗ Peter 1:15-16**—But as he which hath called you is _____, so be ye _____ in all manner of conversation; because it is _____, Be ye _____; for _____ _____ _____.

48

# LESSON 20

## FOLLOWING JESUS

All believers of Christ have a responsibility to be a witness for Jesus. We must tell somebody about the birth, the death and the resurrection of Jesus. We must be in a hurry to be about our Father's business. There are three disciples in this passage who we do not want to pattern our lives after.

Jesus is Lord. How can we tell Him to wait or I have something else that I have to do first. Nothing is more important than being responsible and obedient to do what God has commissioned you to. Let us be about our Father's business and not make him wait on us to complete our earthly assignments. Be obedient to the call of the Spirit.

---

**1. Luke 9:57**—And it came to pass, that, as they went in the way, a certain man said unto him, _____, I will _____ _____ withersoever, _____ _____.

**2. Luke 9:58**—And Jesus said unto him, _____ have holes, and _____ of the _____ have _____; but the _____ of _____ hath not where to lay his head.

**3. Luke 9:59**—And he said unto another, _____ _____. But he said, Lord, suffer me first to go and _____ _____ _____.

**4. Luke 9:60**—Jesus said unto him, _____ _____ _____ _____ _____ _____: but go thou and preach the kingdom of God.

**5. Luke 9:61**—And another also said, Lord, I _____ follow thee; but let me _____ _____ _____ _____ _____, which are at home at my house.

**6. Luke 9:62**—And Jesus said unto him, _____ _____; having put his hand to the plough, and looking back, is fit for the _____ _____ _____.

**7. Matt. 19:27**—Then answered Peter and said unto him, Behold, we have forsaken all, and _____ _____; what shall we have therefore?

**8. Matt. 19:28**—And Jesus said unto them, Verily I say unto you, that ye which have followed me, in the regeneration when the _____ _____ _____ shall sit in the Throne of his glory, ye also shall sit upon twelve thrones, judging the twelve tribes of Israel.

**9. Matt. 19:29**—And every one that hath forsaken _____; or _____, or _____, or father, or mother or wife, or children, or lands, for my sake, shall receive an hundredfold, and shall inherit _____ _____.

# LESSON 21

## GOD THEN, NOW, AND FOREVER

John 1:1—States that in the beginning was the Word and the word was with God and the Word was God. God is the creator of everything, so therefore we are his creation. He created the stars, the sun and even the moon. He did all this by faith. In faith He spoke the world into existence. Rom. 4:17 tells us to call those things which be not as thou they were. We don't have to see in the natural to call things in order in the spirit. In the beginning everything that God wanted to come He said let there be and it was whatever He was calling into the earth's realm. In faith we have that same ability. We need to call something's into the earth's realm.

We don't have to see it just call it. What is it that we need God to do that we are not speaking into existence? Speak it. This same scripture also says that He was the Word. How can we say we love God but don't take time to read his word? His word is how we communicate with him. It is impossible to love God and not study his word. We cannot have a relationship with God and not know His word. The more we apply ourselves to study his Word the more we get to know Him. God is a spirit and if we wish to worship Him we must get in the spirit. God is not going to reveal any of his mysteries to us as long as we have a carnal mind. We must know His word and know that He and The Word are one.

**1. John 1:1**—In the _____ was the _____, and the word was with _____; and the _____ was _____.

**2. John 1:2**—The same was in the _____ with _____.

**3. John 1:3**—All things were made by _____; and without him was not anything made that was _____.

**4. John 1:4**—In him was _____; and the _____ was the light of men.

**5. John 1:5**—And the _____ _____ in _____; and the _____ _____ it not.

**6. John 1:6**—There was a man sent from _____; whose name was _____.

**7. John 1:7**—The same came for a _____; to bear witness of the _____; that all _____ through him _____ _____.

**8. John 1:8**—He was not that _____, but was _____ to _____ _____ of that _____.

**9. John 1:9**—That was the _____ Light, which lighteth every man that cometh into the _____.

**10. John 1:10**—He was in the _____, and the _____ was made by him, and the _____ knew _____ _____.

**11. John 1:11**—He came _____ _____ _____; and his own _____ _____ _____.

**12.   John 1:12**—But as _____ as _____ him, to them gave he _____ to become the _____ of God, even to them that _____ on _____ _____.

**13.   John 1:13**—Which were _____, not of _____; nor of the will of the _____, nor of the will of _____, but of _____.

# LESSON 22

## GODLY COUNCIL FOR ALL

Psalm1:1 tells us that "Blessed is the man that walketh not in the counsel of the ungodly, nor standeth in the way of sinners, nor sitteth in the seat of the scornful." In this life everyone will need someone to talk to. It's alright to get advice or go for counseling but know who is giving the advice. A Christian should never, ever get advice from an ungodly person. How can an ungodly person give a God fearing man or woman of God advice? A person who is not godly will give worldly or carnal advice. If they don't know Jesus it can't be godly advice. Godly advice is the only council that a Christian should be advised to take. Be careful of the advice you take and who it is coming from.

The word of God tells us in the book of Prov. 3:6 "In all thy ways acknowledge him, and he shall direct thy paths." Translation, even in everyday living we should consult the Lord on which way to go and how to do it. We should not only go to God for complex decisions but for all decisions. This passage is instructing believers how to conduct themselves. Believers must mature and grow on grace through the teaching ministry. Also as believers we should help our sisters and brothers mature in the Lord. We all have a part in helping each other to mature to become all we can for the kingdom of God.

---

**1. Titus 2:1**—But _____ thou the things which become _____ _____.

**2. Ti. 2:2**—That the _____ _____ be _____, _____, _____, sound in _____, in _____, in _____.

**3. Ti. 2:3**—The _____ _____ likewise, that they be in behavior as becometh _____, not _____ _____, not given to much _____, teachers of _____ _____;

**4. Ti. 2:4**—That they may _____ the _____ _____ to be _____, to love their _____, to love their _____,

**5. Ti. 2:5**—To be _____, _____, keepers at _____, _____, _____, to their own _____, that the word of _____ be not _____.

**6. Ti. 2:6**—_____ _____ likewise exhort to be _____ _____.

**7. Ti. 2:7**—In all things shewing thyself a pattern of _____ works: In _____ shewing _____, _____; _____,

**8. Ti. 2:8**—_____ _____, that cannot be _____; that he that is of the contrary part may be ashamed, having no _____ thing to say of you.

9. **Ti. 2:9**—Exhort _____ to be _____ unto their own _____, and to please them well in _____ _____; not answering again;

10. **Ti. 2:10**—Not purloining, but shewing all _____ _____; that they may _____ the _____ of _____ _____ _____ in all things.

11. **Ti. 2:11**—For the _____ of _____ that bringeth _____ hath _____ to all _____,

12. **Ti. 2:12**—_____ us that, _____ _____ and _____ _____, we should live _____, _____, and _____, in this _____ _____;.

# LESSON 23

## GRACE

Grace is favor or kindness shown without regard to the worth or merit of the one who receives it and in spite of what that person deserves. Grace is one of the key attributes of God. This attribute of God is what moved Him to save us. It is the unmerited favor of God. We realize that this refers to the fact that man did not deserve to be saved, but God made him the recipient of Salvation anyhow.

The only way of Salvation for any person is through the grace of the Lord Jesus Christ. Paul makes it abundantly clear that Salvation is not something that can be earned; it can be received only as a gift of grace. Grace, however, must be accompanied by faith; a person must trust in the mercy and favor of God, even while it is undeserved.

Although the grace of God is always free and undeserved, it must not be taken for granted. Grace is only enjoyed within the Covenant—the gift is given by God, and the gift is received by people through repentance and faith. Grace is humbly sought through the prayer of faith. We do thank God for the grace. Without the grace of God we could all yet be in our sin on our way to destruction and damnation. We thank God through grace He saved us. "For by **grace** are ye saved **through** faith" (Eph. 2:8).

**1. John 1: 16-17**—And of his fullness have _____ we received, and _____ for _____. For the _____ was given by _____, but _____ and _____ came by _____ _____.

**2. Eph. 2: 5**—Even when we were dead in sins, hath quickened us together with _____, (by grace ye are saved);

**3. Eph. 2: 6**—And hath raised us up together, and made us sit together in _____ places in _____ _____:

**4. Eph. 2: 7**—That in ages to come he might shew the exceeding riches of his _____ in his _____ toward us through _____ _____.

**5. Eph. 2: 8**—For by _____ are ye _____ through _____; and that not of _____: it is the _____ _____ _____:

**6. Acts 15:11**—But we _____ that through the _____ of the _____ _____ _____ we shall be _____, even as they.

**7. Eph. 4:7**—But unto every one of us is _____ _____ according to the _____ of the _____ of _____.

**8. Titus 2:11**—For the _____ of _____ that bringeth _____ hath _____ to all _____.

# LESSON 24

## HOW ARE YOU LIVING?

The Bible does not teach us to be religious neither does the bible teach denomination, but what the Bible does teach is Holy living. Now whether or not we live-it is up to us. The bible teaches us how to love each other and live together here on this earth. If we don't know how to live together here on this earth then for sure we will not be able live together in heaven. Below are two words that we hear all the time but do we really know what they mean? For sure they are not the name of your church or the kind of church you go to but rather how we should suppose to live our lives on a daily basis.

Enough with religion, let us teach that everyone needs a **personal relationship with Jesus Christ**. We need to live this lifestyle before others so that we may draw them in to the fold of Christ. If we are only living it on Sunday then who will follow us? Let us live this lifestyle seven days a week.

**Holy** is moral and ethical wholeness or perfection, freedom from evil. Holiness is one of the essential elements of God's nature required of His people. Holiness may also be rendered "Sanctification" or "Godliness." The Hebrew word for "holy" denotes that which is sanctified or set apart for divine service.

**Sanctification** is the process of God's grace by which the believer is separated from sin and becomes dedicated to God's righteousness.

**1. 1ˢᵗ Pet.1:16**—Because it is written, _____ _____ _____; _____ _____ _____ _____.

**2. John 17:14**—I have given them thy word; and the world hath hated them, because they are not of the world, _____ _____ _____ _____ _____ _____ _____.

**3. John 17:15**—I pray not that thou shouldest take them out of the world, but that thou shouldest _____ _____ _____ _____ _____.

**4. John 17:16**—They are not of the _____, even as I am not _____ _____ _____.

**5. John 17:17**—Sanctify them through thy truth: _____ _____ _____ _____.

**6. John 17:18**—As thou hast sent me into the world, even so have I also _____ _____ _____ the world.

**7. John 17:19**—And for their sakes I _____ myself, that they also might be _____ _____ _____ _____.

**8. 2ⁿᵈ Thess. 2:13**—But we are bound to give thanks alway to God for you, brethren beloved of the Lord, because God hath from the beginning chosen you to _____ _____ _____ of the Spirit and belief of the truth:

**9. 2<sup>nd</sup> Thess. 2:14**—Whereunto he called you by our gospel, to the obtaining of the glory of _____ _____ _____
_____.

**10.   2<sup>nd</sup> Thess. 2:15**—Therefore, brethren, stand fast, and hold the traditions_____ _____ _____ _____,
whether by word, or our epistle.

## LESSON 25

### HOW WILL YOU DECIDE?

God created us so that we can praise Him for He is truly worthy to be praised. Those who are walking after the flesh, they are the ones who take pleasure in things and ways of the world. Those who have concerns with things of the flesh like drinking, lying, stealing, gambling, cheating, adultery, fornication, gossiping just to name a few, are the ones who are yet walking in flesh and not in the spirit of God.

To be carnally minded is the mental inclination of the fallen nature which is death. A carnal mind has all the potential of death just as an overdose of poison. But to be spiritually minded is eternal life and peace. When we have the spirit of God this is our guarantee of life. The mind-set of the flesh is death because it is enmity against God. The mind of the flesh is not subject to the law of God. The mind of the flesh wants what it wants. It wants its own will and not the will of God. We must not allow the enemy to control our mind. How will you decide? Will it be what your flesh wants or what God wants? The word of God tells us to choose ye this day who we are going to serve. We cannot serve two masters. For we will either love one and hate the other. We have to make up our minds who we will serve. We are either going to serve Satan or we are going to serve God. Make the correct decision and I'll see you in heaven.

**1. Rom. 8:5**—For they that are after the flesh do mind the things of the flesh; but they that are after the ＿＿＿＿＿ the things of the Spirit.

**2. Rom. 8:7**—Because the ＿＿＿＿＿ ＿＿＿＿＿ is enmity against God: for it is not subject to the law of God, neither indeed can be.

**3. Rom. 8:8**—So then they that are in the ＿＿＿＿＿ ＿＿＿＿＿ ＿＿＿＿＿ ＿＿＿＿＿.

**4. 1ˢᵗ Pet. 5:8**—Be sober, be vigilant; because your adversary the devil, as a roaring lion, walketh about, seeking whom he may ＿＿＿＿＿:

**5. Rom. 12:2**—And be not conformed to this world: but be ye transformed by the renewing of your mind, that ye may prove what is that good and acceptable, ＿＿＿＿＿ ＿＿＿＿＿, ＿＿＿＿＿ ＿＿＿＿＿ ＿＿＿＿＿.

**6. Philip. 2:5**—Let this mind be in you, which was also in ＿＿＿＿＿ ＿＿＿＿＿.

**7. Eph. 4:23**—And be renewed in the ＿＿＿＿＿ ＿＿＿＿＿ ＿＿＿＿＿ ＿＿＿＿＿;

**8. Eph. 4:24**—And that ye put on the new man, which after God is created in righteousness and ＿＿＿＿＿ ＿＿＿＿＿.

**9. 2ⁿᵈ Cor. 5:17**—Therefore if any man be in Christ, he is a new creature: old things are passed away; behold, ＿＿＿＿＿ ＿＿＿＿＿ ＿＿＿＿＿ ＿＿＿＿＿ ＿＿＿＿＿.

**10.** **1ˢᵗ Cor. 3:16**—Know ye not that ye are the temple of God, and that the Spirit of God _____ _____ _____?

**11.** **1ˢᵗ Cor. 3:17**—If any man defile the temple of God, him shall God destroy; for the temple of God is holy, _____ _____ _____ _____.

# LESSON 26

## JESUS TEACHES THE MODEL PRAYER

The Model Prayer is often called the Lord's Prayer but actually He taught this to the disciples. According to the book of Matthew religious leaders wanted to be recognized as holy and public prayer was one way to get attention. Jesus saw through their self righteous acts and taught that the essence of prayer should not be on public display for attention, yet more of a private communication with God. There is a time when we may have need for a public prayer, but to pray so that men may boast on you and how well you pray, then you are no better than those Pharisees. To God be the glory in everything that we do. God gets no glory from your prayer of "Look at me". To God be the glory in everything we do. God gets no glory from your prayer of "Look at me."

When we pray we should not do as they Pharisee's who just wanted to be seen but yet we should be sincere. It's not how long or how loud but the sincerity of the prayer. God hears the heart but man hears the voice.

---

**1. Matt. 6:6**—But thou, when thou _____, enter into thy closet, and when thou hast shut thy door, _____ to thy _____ which is in _____; and thy _____ which seeth in _____ shall _____ _____ _____.

**2. Matt. 6:7**—But when ye _____, use not _____ repetitions, as the _____ do: for they think that they shall be heard for their much _____.

**3. Matt. 6:8**—Be not ye therefore like unto them: for your _____ knoweth what things ye have need of, _____ ye _____ him.

**4. Matt. 6:9**—After this manner therefore _____ _____: Our Father which _____ _____ _____, _____ be thy _____.

**5. Matt. 6:10**—Thy _____ _____. Thy will be done in earth, _____ _____ _____ _____ _____.

**6. Matt. 6:11**—Give us this _____ _____ _____ bread.

**7. Matt. 6:12**—And _____ us our _____, as we forgive our _____.

**8. Matt. 6:13**—And _____ _____ not into _____, but _____ us from _____: For thine is the kingdom, and the _____, and the _____ for ever _____.

# LESSON 27

## JUSTIFICATION

Man was told not to eat of the tree of the knowledge of good and evil because he would surely die. When they ate thereof, man became guilty. The death sentence was passed upon him. In Romans 8:3, Jesus came in the likeness of sinful flesh, and for sin, condemned sin in the flesh.

The death of Jesus was satisfactory to God in payment for man's sins; therefore man is admitted to justification. As we go over our lesson this will shed more light on justification or the assurance that we have been pardoned, forgiven or released from punishment due from sin. Justification is the process by which sinful human beings are made acceptable to a Holy God.

The term Justification is used in reference to our Creator dying for our sins. Justification, as used in regard to salvation, means an act which pardons or releases one from punishment due for sin or the process by which sinful human beings are made acceptable to a Holy God. Once we receive Jesus Christ as our personal Savior and we are re-born of his Holy Spirit then we are justified through the blood of Jesus. Being justified says that Jesus Christ has paid the penalty for our sins and what He did human or animal could have done. We are no longer guilty but we have been made free and justified through the blood of Jesus Christ. We are not guilty.

**1. Gal. 2:16**—Knowing that a man is not _____ by the works of the law, but by the _____ of Jesus Christ, even we have believed in Jesus Christ, that we might be justified by the faith of Christ, and not by the works of the law: for by the works of the law shall no flesh be justified.

**2. Gal. 2:17**—But if, while we seek to be _____ by Christ, we ourselves also are found _____, is therefore Christ the minister of _____? God forbid.

**3. Gal. 5:4**—Christ is become of no effect unto you, whosoever of you are _____ by the law; ye are fallen from _____.

**4. Rom. 3:20**—Therefore by the deeds of the law there shall no flesh be _____ in his sight: for by the law is the knowledge of _____.

**5. Rom. 8:1**—There is therefore now no _____ to them which are in Christ Jesus, who _____ not after the _____, but after the _____.

**6. Rom. 8:2**—**For** the law of the _____ of life in Christ Jesus hath made me _____ from the law of _____ and death.

**7. Rom. 8:3**—For what the law could not do, in that it was weak through the _____, God sending his own _____ in the likeness of _____ _____, and for sin, _____ _____ in the _____:

**8. Rom. 8:4**—That the _____ of the law might be fulfilled in us, who walk not after the _____, but after the _____.

# LESSON 28

## KEEP PRAISING GOD

Paul was one of my most favorite men of God. He was a teacher, a preacher, an apostle and most of all a servant of Jesus Christ. As a believer Paul went through great persecution, suffering, and opposition. In all that Paul went through he continued to fight the good fight of faith and he yet rejoiced in the Lord. Can we get to that peak in our lives? We need to find that place in God where we will yet praise Him even when the times are bad.

We are not going through nearly as much as the apostle Paul went through as being a Follower of Christ, but he yet found hope and rejoiced in the strength of Jesus Christ. We should have the attitude of Paul. Paul praised God when he had it and Paul praised God when he didn't have it. We should be content in whatever state that we are in. We should learn to be thankful where we are. Praising God for who he is. God wants us to get to a place in Him where we trust Him no matter what. We need to get to that place where we know without a shadow of doubt that God is our supplier of every one of our needs.

When we have no money we should keep praising God. Why? Because we know that He is Jehovah Jireh the God of all my needs. When we are sick in our bodies we should keep praising God. Why? Because we know that He is Jehovah Rapha the God that healeth thee. No matter what the day may bring we are to keep praising God. Why? Because we know that He's in control. You may not see what God has for you now, but you should keep praising God until it comes to pass.

**1. Philip. 4:4**—Rejoice in the _____ alway: and again I say, _____.

**2. Philip. 4:5**—Let your moderation be _____ unto all men. The _____ is at hand.

**3. Philip. 4:6**—Be _____ for _____; but in every thing by _____ and _____ with thanksgiving let your _____ be made _____ unto God.

**4. Philip. 4:7**—And the peace of God, which passeth all _____, shall keep your _____ and minds through _____ _____.

**5. Philip. 4:8**—Finally, brethren, whatsoever things are _____, whatsoever things are _____, whatsoever things are _____, whatsoever things are _____, whatsoever things are _____, whatsoever things are of good _____; if there be any virtue, and if there be any _____, think on these things.

**6. Philip. 4:9**—Those things, which ye have both learned, and _____, and _____, and seen in me, do: and the _____ of _____ shall be with you.

**7. Philip. 4:10**—But I _____ in the _____ greatly, that now at the last your care of me hath flourished again; wherein ye were also _____, but ye lacked opportunity.

**8. Philip. 4:11**—Not that I _____ in respect of want: for I have _____, in whatsoever state I am, therewith to be _____.

**9. Philip. 4:12**—I know both how to be abased, and I know how to _____: everywhere and in all things I am Instructed both to be full and to be _____, both to abound and to _____ need.

**10.   Philip. 4:13**—I _____ _____ _____ _____ through _____ which _____ me.

# LESSON 29

## ONLY ONE GOSPEL

What is the Gospel? The gospel is the joyous good news of salvation in Jesus Christ. The Greek word translated as "gospel" means "a reward for bringing good news" or simply "good news." In Isaiah 40:9, the prophet proclaimed the "good tidings" that God would rescue His people from captivity. The gospel is not a new plan of salvation; it is the fulfillment of God's plan of salvation that was begun in Israel, was completed in Jesus Christ, and is made known by the church.

The gospel is the saving work of God in His Son Jesus Christ and a call to faith in Him (Rom. 1:16-17). Jesus is more than a messenger of the gospel; He is the gospel. The good news of God was present in His life, teaching, and atoning death. Therefore, the gospel is both a historical event and a personal relationship.

**1. Gal. 1:6-7**—I marvel that ye are so soon removed from him that called you into the _____ of _____ unto another gospel: Which is not another; but there be some that trouble you, and _____ _____ the _____ of _____.

**2. Gal. 1:8**—But though we, or an angel from _____, preach any other _____ unto you than that which we have _____ unto you, let him be _____.

**3. Gal. 1:9**—As we said before, so say I now again, If any _____ _____ any other _____ unto you than that ye have _____, let him be _____.

**4. Gal. 1:10**—For do I now persuade _____, or _____? Or do I seek to _____ _____? For if I yet _____ men, I should not be the _____ of _____.

**5. Gal. 1:11-12**—**But** I certify you, brethren that the _____ which was _____ of me is not after _____. For I neither received it of_____, neither was I taught it, but by the _____ of _____ _____.

## LESSON 30

### PARABLE OF THE TARES

This parable is about the wheat which looks identical to the tare. Wheat and tare grow in the same field. Wheat is what the farmer wants but the tare is what grows around the wheat something like a weed. Because the wheat and tare are so identical, it is not good for you to pull up the tare because of the loss you can suffer if it's the wheat.

The Christians that say they know God you will know them by the fruit they bear and the pretend Christians who don't know God you will also know them by the fruit they don't bear. This parable allows us to know that we must all live together (the sinner, the hypocrite and the Christian). We cannot get around them. They are everywhere even in our churches. Do we put them out? No. They are simply imposters in life that pretend to be on a spiritual journey.

God is allowing them to change. Hoping that as they change that there may be a change of their mind and their heart. If not then in the end God will do the separating and in the fire they shall be destroyed.

---

1. Matt. 13: 25—But while men slept, his _____ came and sowed _____ among the _____, and went his way.

2. Matt. 13:26—But when the _____ was sprung up, and brought forth _____, then appeared the _____ also.

3. Matt. 13:27—So the _____ of the householder came and said unto him, Sir, didst not thou _____ good seed in thy _____? From whence then hath it _____?

4. Matt. 13:28—He saith unto them, an _____ hath done this. The servants said unto him, Wilt thou then that we go and _____ _____ _____?

5. Matt. 13:29—But he said, _____; lest while ye gather up the _____ ye root up also the _____ with them.

6. Matt. 13:30—Let _____ grow together until the _____: and in the time of harvest I will say to the _____, Gather ye together first the _____, and bind them in _____ to burn them: but gather the _____ into my barn.

# LESSON 31

## PHILIP PREACHING JESUS CHRIST

Philip, the deacon who later became an Evangelist, is one of the best known Evangelists of the New Testament church. We are not to confuse him with the apostle Philip who is not mentioned by name in the scripture until after the day of Pentecost. This Philip was one of the first seven appointed deacons by the apostles. Philip's duty was to observe the administration of the church community treasury.

The record of Philip's life that is given to us in the scriptures does not indicate a specific calling of God upon Philip to be an Evangelist (Acts 21:8). There is no mention of Philip having a vision or hearing a voice from on high telling him to go preach. Philip preached and did the work of an evangelist because he had a burden to reach the lost souls of mankind. All he needed was an opportunity to expound the gospel to the lost. This should be the concern of every minister of the gospel and every born again believer should witness to others about Jesus at the opportune time.

---

**1. Acts 8:4**—Therefore they that were scattered abroad went everywhere _____ _____ _____.

**2. Acts 8:5**—Then Philip went down to the city of Samaria, and _____ _____ unto them.

**3. Acts 8:6**—And the people with one accord gave heed unto those things which Philip spake, hearing and seeing the _____ which he did.

**4. Acts 8:7**—For unclean spirits, crying with loud voice came out of many that were possessed with them: and many taken with palsies, and that were _____, were healed.

**5. Acts 8:12**—But when they believed Philip _____ the things concerning the _____ _____ _____, and the name of _____ _____, they were _____, both _____ and _____.

**6. Acts 8:26**—And the angel of the Lord spake unto Philip, saying, Arise, and go toward the south unto the way that goeth down from Jerusalem unto Gaza, _____ _____ _____.

**7. Acts 8:35**—Then Philip opened his mouth, and began at the same scripture, and _____ _____ _____ _____.

**8. Acts 8:36**—And as they went on their way, they came unto certain water: and the eunuch said, See, here is water; what doth _____ _____ _____ _____ _____?

**9. Acts 8:37**—And Philip said, If thou believest, with all thine heart, thou mayest. And he answered and said, I _____ _____ _____ _____ is the _____ _____ _____.

**10.   Acts 8:38**—And he commanded the chariot to stand still: and they went down both into the water, both Philip and the eunuch; and he _____ _____.

**11.   Acts 8:39**—And when they were come up out of the water, the Spirit of the Lord caught away Philip, that the eunuch saw him no more: and he went on his way _____.

**12.   Acts 8:40**—But Philip was found at Azotus: and passing through he _____ _____ _____ _____ _____, till he came to Caesarea.

# LESSON 32

## RECONCILIATION

Reconciliation is defined as the act of adjusting friendship, renewing a harmonious relationship, the process by which God and people are brought together again. In Salvation it has reference to restoring one to the harmony and friendliness with God which Adam knew before his fall. God loves the sinner but it is impossible for Him to not to judge the sin. God cannot over look sin nor does He condone it.

Jesus is our reconciler because He removed the stigma that broke the harmony between God and man. The same act which redeemed, justified, and atoned, also reconciled. Of course all of it is only made effective by obedient faith.

The initiative in reconciliation was taken by God—while we were still sinners and enemies, Christ died for us. Reconciliation is thus God's own completed act, something that takes place before human actions such as confession, repentance, and restitution. God Himself has reconciled us to Himself through Jesus Christ.

Through the sacrifice of Christ, people's sins are atoned for and God's wrath appeased. Thus, a relationship of hostility and alienation is changed into one of peace and fellowship. If you don't know Christ in the pardon of your sins this is your time. Acknowledge that you are a sinner and repent and be reconciled back to the Father.

1. **Rom. 5:8**—But _____ commendeth his love toward us, in that, while we were yet _____, _____ died for us.

2. **Rom. 5:9**—Much more then, being now _____ by his _____, we shall be _____ from _____. through him.

3. **Rom. 5:10**—For if, when we were _____, we were _____ to _____ by the _____ of his Son, much more, being _____, we shall be _____ by his _____.

4. **2nd Cor.5:18**—And all things are of _____, who hath _____ us to himself by _____ _____, and hath given to us the _____ of _____;

5. **2nd Cor.5:19**—To wit, that _____ was in _____, _____. the world unto himself, not imputing their _____ unto them; and hath _____ unto us the word of _____.

6. **2nd Cor.5:20**—Now then we are _____ for Christ, as though _____. did beseech you by us: we _____ you in Christ's stead, be ye _____ to _____.

7. **2nd Cor.5:21**—For he hath made him to _____ _____ for us, who knew _____ _____; that we might be made the _____ of _____ _____ _____.

8. **Col. 1:21**—And you, that were sometime _____ and _____ in your _____ by wicked works, yet now hath he _____.

**9. Eph. 2:15**—Having abolished in his flesh the enmity, even the law of _____ contained in ordinances; for to make in himself of twain one _____ _____, so making _____;

**10. Eph. 2:16**—And that he might _____ both unto _____ in one _____ by the _____, having slain the _____ thereby:

# LESSON 33

## REDEMPTION

Before we can understand the Biblical concept of **Redemption** as it applies to Jesus Christ and His death on the cross, we must understand the basic meaning. Like a lot of words within today's church, redemption has come to be used as a specifically religious term. The word Redemption describes God's dealing with mankind. Redemption means deliverance by payment of a price. In the New Testament, Redemption refers to salvation from sin, death and wrath of God by the sacrifice of Christ. Redemption has four basic characteristics.

*1. Bondage*—Something or someone that is not free. The freedom that was available to them was nonexistent or at least, extremely restricted, so that a return to the original state of affairs was required for them to experience freedom, even though that "free" state may still have had limitations imposed that had previously existed before the bondage came about.

*2. Redeemer*—One who would get involved in the liberation of what was in bondage. The redeemer is in more common terms a buyer or a purchaser who must pay a price.

*3. Ransom*—A price paid by the redeemer to cancel the bondage that existed.

*4. Freedom*—What had been in bondage was removed and the individual person or object was restored into its original freedom, its primary state. It doesn't bring a newness of situation but a restoration. This is quite important.

To summarize it all up is: The action of the **Redeemer** who is Jesus Christ, by paying the ransom which was His blood (the Blood of Jesus) affected our freedom with his life the reason we are free today. Yes, we were bought with a price and the price was the blood of Jesus, the blood that Jesus shed on Calvary. Jesus Christ gave his life so that you and I may live.

---

**1. Rom. 6: 18**—Being then made _____ from _____, ye became the _____ of _____.

**2. Rom. 6: 22**—But now being made _____ from _____, and become _____ to God, ye have your _____ unto _____, and the end everlasting life.

**3. 1ˢᵗ Cor. 6:19**—What? Know ye not that your _____ is the _____ of the _____ _____ which is in you, which ye have of _____, and ye are not _____ _____?

**4. 1ˢᵗ Cor. 6:20**—For ye are _____ with a _____: therefore glorify _____ in your _____, and in your _____, which are God's.

**5. 1ˢᵗ Cor. 1:30**—But of him are ye in _____ _____, who of _____ is made unto us _____, and _____, and _____ , and _____:

**6. Titus 2-13:14**—Looking for that blessed hope, and the glorious appearing of the great God and our Savior Jesus Christ; who gave Himself for _____, that he might _____ _____ from all iniquity, and purify unto himself a _____ people, zealous of good works.

**7. 1ˢᵗ Peter 1-18:19** —For as much as ye know that ye were not _____ with _____ things, as silver and gold, from your vain conversation received by tradition from your fathers; But with the _____ _____ of _____, as of a _____ without blemish and without spot:

**8. Col. 1:14**—In whom we have _____ through his _____, even the _____ of _____:

**9. Heb. 9:12**—Neither by the _____ of _____ and _____, but by his own _____ he entered in once into the _____ _____, having obtained eternal _____ for _____.

**10. Heb. 9:13-14**—For if the _____ of _____ and of _____, and the ashes of an _____ sprinkling the unclean, _____ to the purifying of the flesh: How much more shall the _____ of _____, who through the eternal _____ offered himself without spot to God, purge your _____ from dead works to serve the living God?

**11. Heb. 9:15** —And for this cause he is the mediator of the New Testament, that by means of death, for the _____ of the _____ that were under the first testament, they which are called might receive the promise of _____ inheritance.

# LESSON 34

## REGENERATION

Regeneration is the spiritual change brought about in a person's life by an act of God. In regeneration a person's sinful nature is changed and a person is enabled to respond to God in faith. The word regeneration occurs only in the New Testament and it only appears twice (Matt. 19:28 and Titus 3:5), but the concept or idea is common throughout the bible. Whereas justification remits those sins which are past and which occur as a result of our Adamic nature, regeneration deals with the replacement of the Adamic nature by the divine nature, the nature of God.

Regeneration involves an enlightening of the mind, a change of will, and a renewed nature. It extends to the total nature of people, changing their desires restoring them to a right relationship with God. The need for regeneration grows out of humanity's sinfulness. It is brought about through God's initiative. God works in the human heart, and the person responds to God through faith. Thus, regeneration is an act of God through the Holy Spirit, resulting in resurrection from sin to a new life in Jesus Christ.

**1. Matt. 19:28**—And Jesus said unto them, Verily I say unto you, that ye which have _____ me, in the _____ when the _____ _____ _____ shall sit in the throne of his _____, ye also shall sit upon twelve thrones, judging the twelve tribes of Israel.

**2. 2ⁿᵈ Cor. 5:17**—Therefore if _____ _____ be _____ _____, _____ _____ a _____ _____: old _____ are _____ _____; behold, all things are become new.

**3. John 3:15**—That _____ _____ in _____ should not _____, but _____ _____ _____.

**4. John 3:16**—For God **so** _____ the world, that he gave his only _____ _____, that _____ believeth in _____ should not _____, but have _____ _____.

**5. John 3:17** —For God sent _____ _____ _____ into the _____ to _____ the _____; but that the _____ through him _____ be saved.

**6. John 3:18**—He that _____ on him is not _____: but he that _____ not is _____ already, because he hath not believed in the name of the only _____ _____ _____ _____.

**7. Titus 3:5**—Not by works of _____ which we have done, but according to his mercy he _____ _____, by the washing of _____, and _____ of the _____ _____;

**8. Titus 3:6**—Which he shed on us abundantly through _____ _____ _____ _____;

**9. Titus 3:7** —That being _____ by his _____, we should be made _____ according to the hope of eternal life.

# LESSON 35

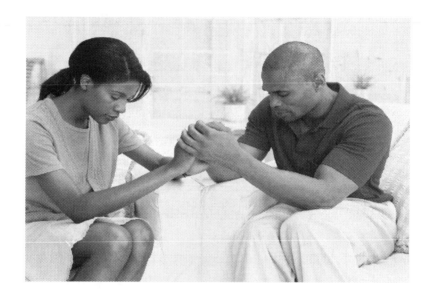

## DOES GOD HEAR A SINNER'S PRAYER?

We are going to allow the scriptures to answer this question. Everybody goes to church. Everybody is quoting scriptures, teaching and preaching but does God really hear their prayer? Does your lifestyle line up with the word of God? Is there a prerequisite that God requires from us in order for our prayers to be heard? Do you think that because we go to church, we give our tithes, and we are morally good people that this validates our prayers to be heard?

We must line up with the word of God, line upon line and precept upon precept. Let us not judge our friends and neighbors but let us examine ourselves. Is God really hearing our prayers or are we walking off the prayers of someone else? Someone like who? It could be by the prayers of your parents, your grandmother, or your great grandmother whom you have never seen. You could be on the prayers of a neighbor from when you were young. Yes, somebody is definitely praying for you or it could just be the grace and mercy of God that is keeping you from danger seen and unseen. When was the last time you were in prayer? Not for a new car or a new house but just to say Lord I thank you. Maybe you are the one that only talks to God when you have a need. How vain. After reading these scriptures examine yourself to find out where you are on the prayer scale.

_____

**1. Is. 59:1**—Behold, the Lord's hand is not _____, that it _____ _____ _____; neither his _____ heavy, that it _____ _____:

**2. Is. 59:2**—But _____ _____ have _____ between _____ and _____ _____, and your _____ have hid his _____ from _____, that he will _____ _____.

**3. Prov. 15:29** The Lord is _____ from the _____: but he _____ the _____ of _____ _____.

4. **John 9:31**—Now we _____ God _____ _____ _____: but if any _____ be a _____ of _____ and doeth his will, _____ _____ _____.

**5. John 15:7**—If ye _____ _____ _____, and my words _____ _____ _____, ye shall _____ what _____ _____, and it shall be done unto you.

**6. Psalm 34:15**—The _____ of the _____ are upon _____ _____, and his _____ are open unto their cry.

**7. Psalm 34:16**—The face of the Lord is _____ them that do _____, to _____ _____ the _____ of them from the _____.

**8. Psalm 34:17**—The _____ _____, and the _____ _____, and _____ them out of all _____ _____.

**9. 1ˢᵗ Pet. 3:7**—Likewise, _____ _____, dwell with them according to knowledge, giving _____ unto the _____, as unto the _____ _____, and as being heirs together of the grace of life; that _____ _____ _____ _____ _____.

**10.  1ˢᵗ Pet. 3:12**—For the _____ of the _____ are over the _____, and his _____ are _____ unto their _____: but the _____ of the _____ is against them _____ _____ _____.

# LESSON 36

## SWEET HOME

This world that we now live in is just our temporary home. We are just pilgrims passing through. The Bible tells us in Matt. 6:19-20 "Lay not up for yourselves treasures upon earth, where moth and rust doth corrupt, and where thieves break through and steal: but lay up for yourselves treasures in heaven, where neighbor moth nor rust doth corrupt, and where thieves do not break through nor steal."

We should not be so focused on the things here on earth but that which is heavenly. For heaven is and should be our ultimate goal. The believers know that they have a permanent home in heaven that one day they will inhabit. This place called earth is just a place that God has chosen for us to learn how to love each other so that we can one day make heaven our permanent abode. Loving each other starts now right here on earth.

---

1. **2nd Tim. 4:6-7**—For I am now ready to be offered, and the time of my departure is at hand. I have _____ a good _____, I have _____ my course, I have kept the _____:

2. **2nd Tim. 4:8**—Henceforth there is laid up for me a _____ of _____, which the _____, the _____ judge, shall give me at that day: and not to me only, but unto all them also that _____ his appearing.

3. **2nd Cor. 5:1**—For we know that if our _____ _____ of this _____ were dissolved, we have a _____ of God, an house not made with _____, _____ in the _____.

4. **2nd Cor. 5:2**—For in this we _____, earnestly desiring to be clothed upon with our _____ which is from _____:

5. **2nd Cor. 5:3**—If so be that being _____ we shall not be found _____.

6. **2nd Cor. 5:4**—For we that are in this _____ do groan, being _____: not for that we would be _____, but _____ upon, that mortality might be _____ up of _____.

7. **2nd Cor. 5:5**—Now he that hath _____ us for the selfsame thing is _____, who also hath given unto us the _____ of the _____.

8. **2nd Cor. 5:6-7**—Therefore we are always _____, knowing that, whist we are at home in the _____, we are _____ from the _____: (For we _____ by _____, _____ by _____):

# LESSON 37

## THE BAPTISM OF JOHN

Before Jesus was the Glorified One or before he had given up the Ghost, his birth had already been announced through the prophets of old of the coming of the Messiah. John was the forerunner of that time to prepare way of the coming of Jesus Christ our Lord and Savior. John the Baptist was the cousin of Jesus.

His mother Elizabeth and the mother of Jesus were cousins. John preached throughout the wilderness to repent for the kingdom of God is at hand. As the conviction of the spirit of God fell on those that heard, they were all baptized one by one.

John was baptizing the people unto repentance. John was preparing the people to get their hearts and minds right for the one who will give them true baptism the baptism of the Holy Ghost and fire. John was doing his thing telling everybody about the one to come. The one to come was Jesus, our Lord and Savior, the Messiah.

---

**1. Matt. 28:18**—And Jesus came and spake unto them, saying, All power is given unto me in _____ and in earth.

**2. Matt. 28:19**—Go ye therefore, and teach all nations, baptizing them in the name of the _____, and of the Son, and of the Holy Ghost:

**3. Matt. 28:20**—Teaching them to observe all things whatsoever I have commanded you: and, lo, I am with you alway, even unto _____ _____ _____ _____ _____. Amen

**4. Mark 1:4**—John did baptize in the wilderness, and preach the _____ of _____ for the _____ _____ _____.

**5. Mark 1:7**—And preached, saying, There cometh one mightier than I after me, the latchet of whose shoes I am not worthy to _____ _____ _____ _____.

**6. Mark 1:8**—I indeed have _____ you with water: but he shall _____ you with the _____ _____

# LESSON 38

## THE BEATITUDES

We are going to talk about the "Beatitudes." The Beatitudes is a sermon that Jesus preached on the Mount. The word Beatitude is a Greek word and the translation is "*Blessed*." The Greek translation of blessed means having spiritual well-being and prosperity, the deep joy of the soul.

The Beatitudes describe the ideal disciple and his rewards both present and future. The person that Jesus describes in this passage has a different quality of character and lifestyle than those outside the Kingdom. These set forth the ideal citizen of the Kingdom of Christ. These are the attributes and characteristics that Christ requires of us.

---

**1. Matt. 5:3**—Blessed are the _____ in spirit: for theirs is the Kingdom of heaven.

**2. Matt. 5:4**—Blessed are they that _____: For they shall be _____.

**3. Matt. 5:5**—Blessed are the _____: For they shall _____ the _____.

**4. Matt 5:6**—Blessed are they which do which do hunger and thirst after _____: for they shall be filled.

**5. Matt. 5:7**—Blessed are the _____: for they shall obtain _____.

**6. Matt. 5:8**—Blessed are the _____ in _____: for they shall see God.

**7. Matt. 5:9**—Blessed are the _____ for they shall be called the _____ _____ _____.

**8. Matt. 5:10**—Blessed are they which are _____ for righteousness sake: for theirs is the _____ _____ heaven.

**9. Matt. 5:11**—Blessed are ye, when men shall _____ _____ and _____ _____, and shall say all manner of evil against you _____, _____ _____ sake.

**10. Matt. 5:12**—Rejoice, and be exceeding _____ for great is your reward in _____: for so persecuted they the _____ which were before you.

## LESSON 39

### THE BIRTH OF JESUS

In this lesson there is a young virgin by the name of Mary who was of Jewish descent. Mary was engaged to a man by the name of Joseph. There were three steps in a Jewish marriage. First, the two families agreed to the marriage. Second, a public announcement was made. Lastly, there was a mutual promise or contract for a future marriage known as **betrothal**.

The woman was said to be espoused to the man. This is similar to engagements today except that their relationship could be broken only through death or divorce. After the betrothal there was a one year wait before the marriage took place.

Before Joseph and Mary came together, she became pregnant with a child. Not just any child, but a unique child, a child of the Holy Ghost. Joseph being just a man didn't know quite what to do. Mary was concerned as well and wondered how in the world can she explain this to her family and friends?

Joseph decided he couldn't go through with the marriage. He didn't want to make a scene so he contemplated divorcing her privately. He thought long and hard about Mary and the situation.

As he lay sleeping the angel of the Lord appeared to him in a dream saying Joseph, thou son of David, fear not to take Mary as your wife. The angel of the Lord said "for that which is conceived in her is of the Holy Ghost. She shall bring forth a Son, and thou shall call his name JESUS. This child that she is caring shall save his people from their sins."

Now all this was done that it might be fulfilled, which was spoken of the Lord by the prophet saying "Behold, a virgin shall be with child, and shall bring forth a son, and they shall call his name Emmanuel, which being interpreted is, God with us."

Then Joseph wakes up from his sleep and did as the angel of the Lord instructed him and he made Mary his wife. Even though he made Mary his wife he yet did not come together with her until after she brought forth her first born son: and he called his name JESUS.

_____

**1. Matthew 1:18**—Now the _____ of _____ _____ was on this wise: When as his mother Mary was espoused to _____, before they came together, she was found with _____ _____ _____ _____.

**2. Matthew 1:19**—Then _____ her husband, being a just man, and not willing to make her a publick example, _____ _____ _____ _____ _____ _____ _____.

**3. Matthew 1:20**—But while he thought on these things, behold, the _____ _____ _____ _____ _____ unto him in a dream, saying, Joseph, thou son of _____, fear not to take unto thee Mary thy _____: for that which is conceived in her is of the _____ _____.

**4. Matthew 1:21**—And she shall bring forth a _____, and thou shalt call his _____ _____: for he shall _____ his people from their _____.

**5. Matthew 1:22**—Now all this was done, that it might be fulfilled which was spoken of the _____ _____ _____ _____ _____;

**6. Matthew 1:23**—Behold, a _____ _____ _____ _____ _____, and shall bring forth a son, and they shall call his name _____, which being interpreted is, _____ _____ _____.

**7. Matthew 1:24**—Then Joseph being raised from sleep did as the angel of the Lord had bidden him, _____ _____ _____ _____ _____ _____.

**8. Matthew 1:25**—And knew her not till she had brought forth her _____ _____: and he called his name _____.

# LESSON 40

## THE CHRISTIAN LIFE

As a Christian we are expected to live according to the ways of the Bible which would be according to the lifestyle of Jesus. There are certain standards that we must be striving everyday of our lives to reach. As Christians we are not perfect people but people maturing daily in the knowledge of Jesus Christ. There are also certain ways that we should not image as Christians. The word of God is giving us some precepts in His word that He expects us to follow. When we have the spirit of Christ we are able to follow these precepts better than those who are just church goers.

A Christian is a follower of Jesus Christ. The word Christian appears three times in the New Testament. The disciples were first called Christians in Antioch (Act 11:26). Agrippa said to Paul, "You almost persuade me to be a Christian" (Acts 26:28). Peter exhorted, "If anyone suffers as a Christian, let him not be ashamed" (1st Pet. 4:16). In each instance, the word Christian assumes that the person called by the name was a follower of Christ. Prior to wearing the name Christian they were called believers (Acts 5:14). Today the word Christian is being used along with disciples, sisters and brothers. The name or title that we wear to identify who we are is not important but what is important is our conduct and behavior under the name that we display.

**1. Col.3:1**—If Ye then be risen with _____, seek those things which are _____, where _____ sitteth on the right hand of _____.

**2. Col. 3:2**—Set your _____ on _____ _____, not on _____ on the _____.

**3. Col. 3:3**—For ye are _____, and your _____ is hid with _____ in _____.

**4. Col. 3:4**—When _____, who is our life, shall appear, then shall ye also appear with _____ in _____.

**5. Col. 3:5**—Mortify therefore your _____ which are upon the earth; _____, _____, _____ _____, _____ Concupiscence, and _____, which is _____:

**6. Col. 3:6**—For which things sake the _____ of _____ cometh on the _____ of _____:

**7. Col. 3:7**—In which ye also _____ some time, when ye _____ in them.

**8. Col. 3:8**—But now ye also put off all these; _____, _____, _____, _____, _____ _____ out of your mouth.

**9. Col. 3:9**—Lie not _____ to _____, seeing that ye have put off the _____ _____ with his _____;

**10. Col. 3:10**—And have put on the _____ _____, which is _____ in _____ after the _____ of him that _____ _____:

**11.** **Col. 3:11**—Where there is neither _____ nor _____, circumcision nor un-circumcision, Barbarian, Scythian, bond _____ _____: but _____ is all, and in all.

**12.** **Col. 3:12**—Put on therefore, as the _____ of _____, _____ and _____, _____ of _____, _____, _____ of _____, _____, _____;

**13.** **Col. 3:13**—_____ one _____, and _____ one _____, if any man have a _____ against any: even as _____ _____ you, so also do ye.

# LESSON 41

## THE HOLY GHOST / THE COMFORTER

Jesus knew His time was coming and He would soon have to give up the Ghost. He wanted to assure the believers and his disciples that even though He may not be with them, that the Father was going to send them a comforter. The comforter would be the Holy Ghost. God knew that the law could not keep us. He knew that if it was not for the Holy Ghost then we would not be able to keep ourselves. We do need the Holy Ghost to abide in us. The Holy Ghost is what will keep us when we want to do wrong. The Holy Ghost is what will teach us, guide us and lead us into truth and righteousness. This is the Holy Ghost that John the Baptist was speaking of.

John the Baptist never tried to take anything away from Jesus. He knew he was the forerunner who was sent to baptize the new converts to repentance. Baptizing them unto repentance was conditioning the heart of the believer to prepare him for the Holy Ghost which was to come. John the Baptist was not the Savior but he was the one to prepare them for salvation through the Savior. The baptism of John was an act of obedience and commitment. John even said in the scriptures (Matt.3:11) that he was baptizing with water but the one to come after him would baptize you with the Holy Ghost and with fire. We should all want the Holy Ghost. Why? This it is a promise and a gift from God. Not just any gift. This is a gift that has benefits. Everlasting benefits. This gift will teach us to love one another as our heavenly Father request of us.

**1. Acts 2:38**—Then Peter said unto them, Repent, and be baptized every one of you in the name of Jesus Christ for the remission of sins, and ye shall receive the _____ _____ _____ _____ _____.

**2. John 14:16**—And I will pray the Father, and he shall give you _____ _____, that he may _____ with you forever.

**3. John 14:26**—But the _____, which is the _____ _____, whom the Father will send in my name, he shall teach you all things and bring all things to your remembrance, whatsoever I said unto you.

**4. John 16:7**—Nevertheless I tell you the truth; it is expedient for you that I go away: for if I go not away, the _____ _____ _____ _____ _____ _____; but if I depart, I will send him unto you.

**5. Acts 11:16**—Then remembered I the word of the Lord, how that he said, John indeed baptized with water; but ye shall be _____ _____ _____ _____ _____.

**6. Mark 1:8**—I indeed have baptized you with water: but he shall _____ _____ _____ _____ _____ _____.

**7. Acts 2:4**—And they were all filled with the _____ _____, and began to speak _____ _____ _____, as the Spirit gave them utterance.

**8. Acts 10:44**—While Peter yet spake these words, the _____ _____ fell on all them which heard the word.

**9. Acts 10:45**—And they of the circumcision which believed were astonished, as many as came with Peter, because that on the Gentiles also was poured out the _____ _____ _____ _____ _____.

**10. Acts 10:46**—For they heard them _____ _____ _____, and magnify God. Then answered Peter,

**11. Acts 10:47**—Can any man forbid water, that these should not be _____, which have received the _____ _____ as well as we?

**12. Acts 10:48**—And he commanded them to be _____ the name of the Lord. Then prayed they him to tarry certain days.

# LESSON 42

## THE INWARD STRUGGLES

The Apostle Paul tells us about the struggles that he was having with his flesh. Don't take this wrong, Paul was not the only person having a problem with his flesh. He just happens to be the one giving the testimony. Believers all throughout the Bible have had struggles with their flesh. Even today we yet struggle. This struggle goes on with the believer as well as the unbeliever. No one is exempt. Just as Paul stated even when we want to do good evil is always present. The things that I can do, that is what I allow not. Once we accept Christ the struggle between two natures begin. The natures are of good and evil.

Paul was just like a lot of us and that is trying to fight sin in our own strength. Notice how Paul spoke, everything was I, me, my and myself. He was not allowing the Holy Spirit to keep him but instead he was trying to be kept by the law. We cannot fight sin in our own strength. Instead of trying to overcome sin with our human will power, we must take hold of the power of God's provision for victory over sin. Jesus sent the Holy Ghost to abide in us and us in Him. The Holy Ghost is what keeps us and not we ourselves. We should give our lives to Jesus. This won't completely stop the struggle but you will have the Holy Spirit to help you fight the temptations of this world. Remember you cannot do it in your own strength. We need the Holy Spirit.

**1. Rom. 7:15**—For that which I do I allow not: for what I would, that do I not; _____ _____ _____ _____ , _____ _____ _____ .

**2. Rom. 7:16**—If then I do that which I would not, I consent unto the _____ _____ _____ _____ _____ .

**3. Rom. 7:17**—Now then it is no more I that do it, but sin that _____ _____ _____ .

**4. Rom. 7:18**—For I know that in me (that is, in my flesh,) dwelleth no good thing: for to will is present with me; but how to perform that _____ _____ _____ _____ _____ _____ .

**5. Rom. 7:19**—For the good that I would I do not: but the evil which I _____ _____ , _____ _____ _____ .

**6. Rom. 7:20**—Now if I do that I would not, it is no more I that do it, _____ _____ _____ _____ _____ _____ .

**7. Rom.7:21**—I find then a law, that, when I would do good, _____ _____ _____ _____ _____ .

**8. Rom. 7:22-23**—For I delight in the law of _____ _____ _____ _____ _____ : But I see another law in my members, warring against the law of my mind, and bringing me into captivity to the law of _____ _____ _____ _____ _____ .

**9. Rom 7:24**—O wretched man that I am! _____ _____ _____ _____ _____ _____ _____ _____ _____ _____?

**10.** **Rom 7:25**—I thank God through Jesus Christ our Lord. So then with the mind I myself serve the law of God; _____ _____ _____ _____ _____ _____ _____.

# LESSON 43

## The Inception

---

**1. Rom. 5:12 says** "Wherefore, as by one man _____ entered into the world and death by _____; and so death passed upon all _____, for all have _____":

**2. In question no. 1**—Wherfore, as by one man sin entered into this world—what is the name of the man this statement speaking of? _____

**3. According to Rom.5:12**—man is not punished because of Adam's sin, but, rather, for his own sin. This verse states, Therefore, just as sin entered the world through man and death through sin and in this way death came to all men

**Because All Have S_____d.**

We **inherited** Adam's nature at birth but we **inherit** Christ's nature in the New-Birth (conversion).

**4. Rom.6:12**—Let not _____ therefore reign in your mortal body, that ye should _____ it in the _____ thereof.

**5. Rom. 6:13**—Neither yield ye your _____ as instruments of _____ unto sin: but yield yourselves unto _____, as those that are alive from the _____, and your members as _____ of _____ unto _____.

**6. Rom.6:14**—For _____ shall not have _____ over _____: for ye are _____ under the _____, but under _____.

**7. Rom. 6:15**—What then? Shall _____ _____, because we are not under the _____, but under _____" God forbid.

**8. Eph.2:8**—For by _____ are ye _____ through _____; and that not of _____: it is the _____ of _____:

**9. Rom.6:16**—Know ye not, that to whom ye yield _____ servants to _____, his servants ye are to whom ye obey; whether of _____ unto death, or of obedience unto _____?

**10. Rom.6:17**—But God be thanked, that ye were the _____ of sin, but ye have obeyed from the _____ that form of _____ which was delivered you.

# LESSON 44

## THE SEVEN LAST STATEMENTS OF CHRIST

There were seven last statements of Christ before his crucifixion. These words are shared in churches everywhere during the Easter and Passover celebration. The words were:

1—"Father forgive them, they know not what they do." Those who crucified Jesus were not really aware of what they were doing because they did not recognize Him as the Messiah. Their ignorance of the truth did not mean that they did not deserve forgiveness. Jesus yet showed compassion even in His dying hour.

2—"This day thou shalt be with me in paradise." Jesus is assuring one of the malefactors that he would be with him in heaven.

3—"Woman behold thy son." Jesus is giving the care of his mother to his dear friend John. When Jesus died John took the mother of Jesus into his home. Again even in his death Jesus showed compassion.

4—"My God, my God, why hast thou forsaken me?" Jesus is expressing abandonment.

5—"I thirst." Here He was expressing a natural need but was given vinegar instead.

6—"It is finished." His work was over here on this earth.

7—"Into thy hands I commend my spirit." Indicating that He was about to die and He was about to be that perfect sacrifice that the world needed to live.

---

**1. Luke 23:34**—Then said _____, _____, _____ _____; for they know not what they do. And they _____ his raiment, and _____ _____.

**2. Luke 23:43**—And _____ said unto him, Verily I say unto thee, To day _____ _____ _____ with me in _____.

**3. John 19:26**—When _____ therefore saw his _____ and the _____ standing by, whom he _____, he saith unto his _____, _____, _____ _____ _____!

**4. John 19:28**—After this, _____ knowing that all things were now accomplished, that the _____ might be fulfilled, saith, _____ _____.

**5. Matt. 27:46**—And about the _____ _____ _____ cried with a loud voice, saying Eli, Eli, la-ma-sa-bach-tha-ni? That is to say, _____ _____, _____ _____, _____ _____ _____ _____ _____?

**6. John 19:30**—When _____ therefore had received the _____, he said _____ _____ _____: and he _____ his _____, and _____ _____ _____ _____.

**7. Luke 23:46**—And when _____ had _____ with a loud voice, he said, _____, into thy hands _____ _____ my _____: and having said thus, _____ _____ _____ _____ _____.

# LESSON 45

## THE TEMPTATION OF CHRIST

This lesson is going to teach you that if Satan tempted Jesus Christ, then who are we that he won't tempt us. Satan came with proposals to get Jesus to bow down to him. But how can you offer somebody something that they already own? Psalm 24:1 says "The **earth is the LORD's**, and the fulness thereof; the world, and they that dwell therein." How can you offer the Creator his creation?

The word of God tells us that man shall not live by bread alone, but by every word of God. Reading, studying, meditation, prayer and fasting is the only way we are going to ever be able to resist the temptation of Satan. We need the word of God to abide in us. We can only fight Satan with the word of God. But if we have no word in us then we will succumb to the wiles of the devil every time. We need to eat and digest more of the word of God and less natural digesting. Every time Satan came at Jesus, Jesus had a word for him. If Satan comes at you do you have a word for him? We can't always say that "the devil is a lie" for everything. As long as we live we will always be tempted of Satan. As long as you live you need the word of God. The word is the weapon of choice.

**1. Luke 4:1**—And Jesus being full of the _____ _____ returned from Jordan, and was led by the _____ into the _____.

**2. Luke 4:2**—Being _____ tempted of the _____. And in those days he did eat nothing: and when they were ended, he afterward _____.

**3. Luke 4:3**—And the _____ said unto him, if thou be the _____ _____ _____, command this stone that it be made bread.

**4. Luke 4:4**—And Jesus answered him, saying, _____ _____, That _____ _____ _____ live by bread alone, but by _____ _____ _____ _____.

**5. Luke 4:5**—And the _____, taking him up into an high _____, _____ unto him all the kingdoms of the world in a moment of time.

**6. Luke 4:6**—And the devil said unto him, _____ _____ _____ _____ _____ _____ _____, and the glory of them: for that is delivered unto me; and to whomsoever I will I give it.

**7. Luke 4:7**—If thou therefore wilt _____ _____, all shall be thine.

**8. Luke 4:8**—And Jesus answered and said unto him, _____ _____ _____ _____, _____: for it is written, Thou shalt worship the Lord thy God, and him only shalt thou serve.

**9. Luke 4:9**—And he brought him to Jerusalem, and set him on a pinnacle of the temple, and said unto him, if thou be the _____ _____ _____, cast thyself down from hence:

**10.** **Luke 4:10**—For it is written, He shall give his angels charge over thee, _____ _____ _____:

**11.** **Luke 4:12**—And Jesus answering said unto him, _____ _____ _____, _____ _____ _____ _____ _____ _____ _____ _____.

**12.** **Luke 4:13**—And when the devil had ended all the _____, he departed from him for a _____.

# LESSON 46

## WE MUST FORGIVE

Jesus tells us in His word that we must forgive each other. If we refuse to forgive others our God will not forgive us. When we don't forgive others, we are saying that we don't need God to forgive us. Forgiving others is not for the other person, but for you. You will be judged by God if you refuse to forgive your sister and brother in or out of the Lord. Forgiveness comes from the heart and not from the lips. The lips speak but the heart gives. God is not listening to those words but He is looking at our hearts. Our hearts need to be pure if we want to see Jesus. Forgiveness demonstrates love and maturity in the Jesus. Forgiveness shows God that you are ready for the next level. Don't allow what others have done to you to keep you stagnate because you won't forgive. Let it go and grow.

---

**1. Matt. 6:14**—For if ye _____ men their trespasses, your heavenly Father will also _____ you:

**2. Matt. 6:15**—But if ye _____ not _____ their trespasses, neither will your Father _____ your trespasses.

**3. Matt.18:21**—Then came Peter to him and said, Lord, how oft shall my brother sin against me, and I _____ him? till seven times?

**4. Matt. 18:22**—Jesus saith unto him, I say not unto thee. Until seven times: but, Until _____ _____ _____.

**5. Mark 11:25**—And when ye stand praying, forgive, if ye have _____ against any; that your Father also which is in heaven may _____ _____ _____ _____.

**6. Luke 17:3**—Take heed to yourselves: If thy brother _____ against thee, _____ him; and if he _____ him.

**7. Luke 17:4**—And if he _____ against thee seven times in a day, and _____ times in a _____ turn again to thee, saying, _____ _____; thou shalt _____ _____.

# LESSON 47

## WHAT IS AND IS NOT FAITH?

Hebrews 11:1 says "Now Faith is the substance of things hoped for, the evidence of things not seen". Translation—faith is the expected things that we don't see today with our natural eyes but we believe in our heart that God can and God will bring these expected things into existence on the morrow. Faith is trusting in God, believing God, having confidence in God for this thing that we have hoped for to now show up or to now appear.

Faith is when you don't know how but you believe that God can. Faith is when you don't know when but you believe that God is in control. Faith believes God for the possible when man says it's impossible. Faith is not giving up on your dreams when all the odds are against you because you believe God. Faith is when you continue to hold on to the dream that God has promised even when you don't see it no kind of a way. The evidence will be your promise manifest right before those who said it's not possible. What do you see? Start believing God for what you see in the Spirit but at this time it is not visible.

---

1. **Rom. 14:23**—And he that _____ is damned if he eat, because he _____ not of _____: for whatsoever is not of Faith is sin.

2. **Rom. 10:17**—So then Faith cometh by hearing, and _____ by the _____ _____ _____.

3. **Habakkuk 2:4**—Behold, _____ _____ which is lifted up is not _____ in _____: but the just shall live by Faith.

4. **Rom. 5:1**—Therefore being justified by Faith, we _____ _____ with _____ through our Lord Jesus Christ.

5. **Heb. 11:6**—But without Faith it is impossible to please him (God): for he that _____ to _____ must _____ that he is, and that he is a _____ of them that diligently _____ _____.

6. **James 2:20**—But wilt thou _____, _____ _____ _____, _____ Faith without works is dead?

7. **Eph. 2:8-9**—For by grace are ye saved through Faith; and that not of _____: it is the _____ _____ _____: not of works, lest any man _____ _____.

8. **2ⁿᵈ Thes. 3:2**—and that we may be delivered from _____ and _____ _____: For all men have not Faith.

9. **Rom. 12:3**—For I say, through the grace given unto me, to every man that is among you, not to _____ of _____ more _____ than he ought to think; but to think _____, according as God hath dealt to every man the measure of Faith.

10. **James 5:15**—And the prayer of Faith shall save the sick, and the Lord shall raise him up; and if he hath _____ _____ they _____ be forgiven him.

## LESSON 48

## WHAT IS SIN?

Sin is an act, thought, or way of moral conduct that goes against the law or teachings of God. Sin is to commit moral or ethical offenses. Sin is lawlessness or transgression of God's will, either by omitting to do what God's law requires or by doing what it forbids. What is transgression? Transgression is wrongdoing, misbehavior, disobedience, noncompliance and offense. All of these things are against God.

Transgression or sin can occur in a thought, in our words or in our deeds. Every since that day in the Garden of Eden when the serpent beguiled (deceived) Eve there has been a spiritual war, between God and Satan. The book of Joshua tells us that we have to choose this day who we will serve. This day meaning right now, because tomorrow may be too late. Satan knows that his time is almost up. His goal is to take as many to hell with him as possible.

Sin comes to send the soul to damnation. Sin is an enemy of God. When we sin we grieve the spirit of God. The more we walk after the Holy Spirit the less we will cater to the sins of the world. The time has come for us to stop practicing sin and walk in the ways of holiness and righteousness. We cannot continue to purposely sin and say that we are a friend of God.

1. **1ˢᵗ John 3:4**—Whosoever committeth sin transgresseth also the
_____: for _____ is the _____ of the _____.

2. **Eph. 6:12**—For we _____ not _____ flesh and blood,
but against _____, _____ powers, against the _____
of the _____ of this world, against _____ _____ in
high places.

3. **John 3:16**—For _____ _____ _____ the world,
that he _____ his _____ _____ _____,
that whosoever believeth in him should not _____, but have
_____ _____.

4. **Matt. 6:24**—No _____ _____ _____ two
_____: for either he will _____ the _____, and
_____ the _____; or else he will hold to the one, and
_____ the other. Ye cannot serve _____ _____
_____.

5. **Rev. 20:15**—And whosoever was not _____ written in the
book of _____ was _____ into the _____ _____
_____.

6. **Psalm 51:1**—Have mercy upon me, O God, _____ to thy
_____: according unto the multitude of thy tender mercies
_____ out my _____.

7. **Psalm 51:2**—Wash me thoroughly from mine _____, and
_____ me from _____ _____.

**8. Psalm 51:3**—For I acknowledge my _____: and my sin is ever before me.

**9. Psalm 51:4**—Against thee, thee only have I _____, and done this _____ in thy _____: that thou mightiest be _____ when thou speakest, and be clear when thou judgest.

# LESSON 49

## THE SHEEP AND THE SHEPHERD

Sheep are totally dependent upon the shepherd who tends them with care and compassion. Shepherds were the providers, guides, protectors and constant companions of sheep. Shepherds were inseparable from their flocks. The shepherd would lead the sheep to safe places to graze and then make them lie down for several hours in a shady place. Then as night fell, the shepherd would lead the sheep to the protection of a sheepfold. To get a clear picture of Jesus' meaning in this statement, it is helpful to understand a little of that ancient culture, especially of sheep and shepherding.

Of all domesticated animals, sheep are the most helpless. Sheep will spend their entire day grazing wandering from place to place never looking up. As a result, they often become lost. Sheep have no homing instinct as other animals do. They are totally incapable of finding their way to their sheepfold even when it is in plain sight. By nature, sheep are followers. You know how we follow? If a member say's "I don't like our pastor or our church and I am leaving", there you go, leaving with them. If the lead sheep steps off a cliff, the others will follow.

Sheep are dependent upon the shepherd who tends them with care and compassion or one who will lead them off a cliff. Sound familiar.

---

**1. John 21:15**—So when they had dined, Jesus saith to Simon Peter, Simon, son of Jonas, lovest thou me more than these? He saith unto him _____, _____; thou knowest that I _____ _____, He saith unto him, _____ my _____.

**2. John 21:16**—He saith to him again the _____ _____, Simon, son of _____, _____ _____ _____? He saith unto him. _____, _____; thou knowest that I love thee. He saith unto him Feed my _____.

**3. Matt. 28:19**—Go ye therefore, and _____ all nations, _____ them in the _____ of _____ _____, and of the _____, and of the _____ _____:

**4. Matt. 28:20**—_____ them to _____ all things whatsoever I have _____ _____: and, lo, I am _____ _____ _____, even unto the end of the world. _____.

**5. Psalm 23:1**—The Lord _____ _____ _____; I shall _____ _____.

**6. Matt. 25:32**—And before him shall be _____ all nations: and he shall _____ them one from another, as a _____ divideth his _____ from the _____:

**7. Matt. 25:33**—And he shall set the _____ on _____ _____ _____, but the _____ on the _____.

**8. John 10:2**—But he that _____ in by the door is the _____ of the _____.

**9. John 10:4**—And when he putteth forth his _____ _____, he goeth before them, and the sheep, _____ _____: for they _____ _____ _____.

**10.  John 10:5**—And a _____ will they not _____, but will flee from him: for they _____ not the _____ of _____.

**11.  John 10:7**—Then said _____ unto them again, Verily, verily, I say unto you, _____ _____ _____ _____ of the _____.

**12.  John 10:14**—I am the _____ _____, and know my _____, and am known of mine.

# LESSON 50

## OUR GREATEST INVESTMENT

Let's talk about planning for our future. As one of today's pastors, I've noticed that we don't like to plan for our future. We like to stay in the now. I know the word of God tells us to take "no thought for the morrow." But that verse is speaking of material things or things in the natural. I am speaking of planning in the spiritual for our soul. Has anybody noticed or had concern for all those people who are outside the church and have no desire to come in? For whatever the reason may be why are they not in the church? It is our responsibility to persuade them that they are out of the ark of safety.

This lesson is going to teach us about investing, the investment of our soul. Where will our soul spend eternity? How important is my soul? The time is now because the later may be here sooner than you think. Let's not put off today for later. I want this lesson to teach us that we need to care about our souls more than we care about our houses, cars, boats, truck, and money. For these are material things and they will not last. They are only temporary. Invest in your soul by going to church, reading your bible, fasting, praying and meditating on the Lord's goodness.

**1. Je. 3:15**—And I will give you _____ according to mine _____, which _____ _____ _____ with knowledge _____ _____.

**2. He. 10:25**—Not _____ the _____ of _____ together, as the manner of some is; but _____ one _____: and so much the more, as ye see the day approaching.

**3. Rom. 10:14**—How then shall they call on him in whom they have not _____? And how shall they _____ in him of whom they have _____ _____? And how shall _____ _____ _____ _____ _____?

**4. Joshua 24:15**—And if it seem _____ unto you to serve the _____, _____ _____ this _____ _____ ye _____ _____; whether the gods which your fathers served that were on the other side of the flood, or the gods of the Amorites, in whose land ye dwell: but as for me and _____ _____, _____ _____ _____ _____ _____ _____.

**5. Matt. 10:28**—And fear not them which _____ _____ _____, but are not able to _____ _____ _____: but rather fear him which is able to _____ _____ _____ and _____ _____ _____.

**6. Matt. 6:19**—Lay not up for yourselves _____ _____ _____, where _____ and _____ _____, and where _____ _____ _____ and _____:

**7. Matt. 6:20**—But _____ up for _____ _____ in _____, where neither _____ nor _____ doth _____, and where _____ do not _____ through _____ _____.

**8. 2ⁿᵈ Cor. 4:18**—While we look not at the things which _____ _____, _____, but at the things _____ _____ _____ _____: for the things which are _____ are _____; but the things which are _____ _____ _____ _____.

**9. Prov. 9:10**—The fear of the _____ is the _____ of _____: and the _____ of the _____ is _____.

**10. Phil. 2:12**—Wherefore, my _____, as ye have always _____, not as in my _____ only, but now much more in my absence, _____ _____ _____ _____ _____ _____ _____ and _____.

# LESSON 51

## WE ARE CHOSEN

In this lesson Peter starts off by saying that we are lively stones. What do you think he means here with the word lively stones? God gave Peter that analogy of the stones because the stones represent us, the believers and followers of Jesus Christ.

A builder selects materials and has them delivered to the job site for the construction of a project. In a similar way, God chose us for the construction of His project and His project was the church. He decided to use us for His building of the Kingdom of God. We are the stones of his spiritual kingdom.

The Kingdom of God is built up of all believers and followers of Christ. Back in the days of the Old Testament they used the finest to build the temple. Our church today has that same thing in common with the temples of old. They used the finest of stones to build a lifeless building. God is still using today the finest of his followers to bring life to his Kingdom. If man uses the best to build a lifeless building how much more would God use us with life to magnify his name in the Kingdom of God?

Jesus is the chief corner stone and we are just chips off the block. We are a lively stones, chosen and precious, acceptable to God by Jesus Christ.

**1. 1ˢᵗ Pet. 2:4**—To whom coming, as unto a _____ _____, disallowed indeed of men, but _____ of _____, and _____,

**2. 1ˢᵗ Pet. 2:5**—Ye also, as _____ _____, are built up a _____ _____, an _____ priesthood, to _____ up spiritual sacrifices, acceptable to _____ by _____ _____.

**3. 1ˢᵗ Pet. 2:6**—Wherefore also it is _____ in the _____, Behold, I lay in _____ a _____ _____ _____, elect, precious: and he that believeth on him shall not be _____.

**4. 1ˢᵗ Pet. 2:7**—Unto you therefore which _____ he is _____: but unto them which be _____, the stone which the _____ _____, the same is made the head of the corner.

**5. 1ˢᵗ Pet. 2:8**—And a _____ _____ _____, and a rock of _____, even to them which stumble at the word, being _____: whereunto also they were appointed.

**6. 1ˢᵗ Pet. 2:9**—But ye are a _____ _____, a royal _____, an _____ _____, a _____ _____; that ye should shew forth the praises of him who hath called you out of _____ into his _____ _____:

# LESSON 52

## Our Weapons Are Not Carnal

This lesson is teaching us what weapons to choose for this spiritual warfare that we are engaged in. From the moment that we accepted Jesus Christ as our personal Savior the devil has been on our trail trying to snatch us back. We have to take our post, stand guard and speak the truth against the lies of Satan. We are to proclaim the gospel no matter how much resistance we receive. We are not to waiver in our faith, no matter how strongly we are attacked. Our ultimate defense is the assurance we have of our salvation, an assurance that no spiritual force can take away without a fight.

Our weapon of defense is, not our own opinions and feelings but the Word of God. We are to follow Jesus' example in recognizing that spiritual victories are only possible through prayer and the word of God. Observe how Jesus handled direct attacks from Satan when He was being tempted by him in the wilderness (Matt. 4:1-11). Each temptation was answered the same way and that was with the word of God. If we don't put on the whole armor of God then we have already been defeated. What is the whole armor of God? The whole armor of God is Truth, Righteousness, The Gospel of Peace, Faith, Salvation and the Word of God. Jesus' choice of weapons is our ultimate example for spiritual warfare and that is the word of God.

**1. Eph. 6:10**—Finally, my brethren, be _____ in the Lord, and in the _____ of his _____.

**2. Eph. 6:11**—Put on the _____ _____ of God, that ye may be able to _____ _____ the wiles of _____ _____.

**3. Eph. 6:12**—For _____ _____ not _____ flesh and _____, but against _____, against _____, against the _____ of the _____ of this world, against _____ _____ in _____ _____.

**4. Eph. 6:13**—Wherefore take unto you the _____ armor of _____, that ye may be able to _____ in the evil day, and _____ _____ _____, _____ _____.

**5. Eph. 6:14**—Stand therefore, having your loins girt about with _____, and having on the _____ of _____;

**6. Eph. 6:15**—And your _____ _____ with the preparation of _____ _____ of _____;

**7. Eph. 6:16**—Above all, taking the _____ _____ _____, wherewith ye shall be able to _____ all the _____ _____ of the _____.

**8. Eph. 6:17**—And take the _____ _____ _____, and the _____ of the _____, which is the word of _____:

**Abased**—1. Paul said I know how to be abased meaning he knew how to by with having the bare necessities of life. He knew what it was to have the bread but no meat for a sandwich. 2. It also means to make somebody feel belittled or degraded. 3. In a way that lowers your sense of dignity or self esteem.

**Abolished**—to outlaw something, to put an end to something such as a law.

**Abominable**—1. loathsome, extremely unacceptable or offensive 2. extremely and very unpleasant to experience or very bad quality.

**Abomination**—1. something horrible, an object of intense disapproval or dislike. 2. something that is immoral, disgusting, or shameful, 3. something shameful, intense dislike, hate, a feeling of intense disapproval toward somebody or someone. 4. anything that offends the spiritual religious or moral sense of a person and causes extreme disgust, hatred, or loathing.

**Abound**—1. when you have given to you more than you need at that given time. 2. be plentiful. 3. to be well supplied.

**Abundantly**—1. plentiful, present in great quanties, 2. well supplied, providing a more than plentiful supply of something.

**Accursed**—1. horrible or hateful 2. doomed, enduring the effects of a curse or anything that a curse has pronounced.

**Admonished**—1. to rebuke somebody mildly but being honest about it. 2. to advise somebody to do or, more often not to do something.

**Adorn**—to decorate or beautify.

**Adversary**—one who opposes or hinders another.

**Afflicted** or **Affliction**—1. cause distress, to cause severe physical or mental distress to somebody 2. any condition or problem that produces suffering or pain.

**Anger**—1. a strong feeling of grievance and displeasure 2. to become or make somebody extremely annoyed.

**Apostle**—1. a special messenger of Jesus, 2. a person who Jesus delegated authority for certain task. 3. in the New Testament the apostle would go from town to town establishing and overseeing the church of God as he was led by the Holy Ghost. Jesus started out with twelve apostles. These twelve went out into the world preaching, teaching, witnessing, baptizing, establishing churches, overseeing churches, and ordaining others into the ministry.

**Appeasement**—1. the political strategy of pacifying a potentially hostile nation in the hope of avoiding war, often by granting concessions. 2. an attempt to stop complaints or reduce difficulties by making concessions.

**Atonement**—the act by which God restores a relationship of harmony and unity between Himself and human beings.

**Backbiters**—to speak evil of someone to another and not to the person.

**Banqueting**—1. a lavish meal; feast. 2. a ceremonious public dinner, as to honor a person or benefit a charity.

**Baptism or Baptize**—1. to baptize is the submerging of a new convert into an anointed body of water. 2. baptize is to identify you as a believer of Jesus Christ. 3. baptize is an outer expression of an inner change. To baptize is to publicly announce that you are a Christian and a follower of Christ.

**Barbarian**—1. uncivilized person.2. uncultured person,. somebody with no interest in culture 3. aggressive person, an extremely aggressive or violent person.

**Beatitudes**—the eight declarations of blessedness made by Jesus at the beginning of the Sermon on on the Mount (Matt. 5:3-12), each beginning with "Blessed are."

**Belial**—an Old Testament term designating a person as godless or lawless. Belial sometimes takes the form of a proper name applied to a demon or to Satan. Many scholars believe that Belial is another name for Satan.

**Beseech**—1. to beg somebody. to ask earnestly or beg somebody to do something. 2. beg for something or to ask urgently for something.

**Betrothal**—a mutual promise or contract for a future marriage. In Hebrew custom betrothal was actually part of the marriage process. A Jewish betrothal could be dissolved only by the man's giving the woman a certificate of divorce. Betrothal was much more closely linked with marriage than our modern engagement. But the actual marriage took place only when the bride groom took the bride to his home and the marriage was consummated in the sexual union.

**Blaspheme or Blasphemy**—the act of cursing, slandering, reviling or showing contempt or lack of reverence for God. Christians are commanded to avoid behavior that blasphemes the Lord's name and teaching (1st Tim. 6:1).

**Boaster**—1. overemphasize possessions or accomplishments. 2. excessively proud statements.

**Bondage**—1. slavery, the condition of being enslaved or the practice of being tied up or restrained. 2. the condition of being controlled by something or someone.

**Carnal**—sensual, worldly, non-spiritual; relating to or given to the crude desires and appetites of the flesh or body.

**Charity**—love for others, especially as a Christian virtue.

**Chaste**—1. abstaining from sex on moral grounds. 2. not having extramarital sexual relations 3. pure in thought and deed.

**Christian**—a follower and believer of Jesus Christ. One who believes in the teaching and preaching of the gospel. The disciples were first called Christians in Antioch (Acts 11:26).

**Circumcision**—the surgical removal of the foreskin of the male sex organ. this action served as a sign of God's Covenant relation with His people.

**Comforter**—The Holy Ghost

**Commandments**—a law, a proclamation, a decree or statute;

**Commend**—1. to praise somebody or something. 2. cause something to be acceptable.

**Communion**—fellowship; Lord's Supper

**Condemnation or Condemned**—1. to consider somebody guilty. 2. to judge that somebody or something is to blame for something.

3. to state that somebody or something is in some way wrong or unacceptable. prove somebody guilty.

**Confess**—admit having done something wrong.

**Conformed**—1. to act in accordance or harmony; comply to rules: 2. to act in accord with the prevailing standards, attitudes, practices.3. behave or think in a socially acceptable or expected way.

**Conscience**—1. the sense of what is right and wrong that governs somebody's thoughts and actions, urging him or her to do right than wrong. 2. behavior according to what your sense of right and wrong tells you is right.

**Convocation**—1. a large formal assembly. 2. the arranging or calling of a formal meeting. an assembly of the clergy.

**Countenance**—1. somebody's face, or the expression on it. 2. composure or self control.

**Covenant**—1. a solemn agreement that is binding on all parties. 2. an agreement between two people or to groups that involves promises on the part of each to the other.

**Covetousness**—an intense desire to possess something or someone that belongs to another person.

**Deceit**—the act or practice of deceiving or misleading somebody.

**Defile**—1. to corrupt or ruin something. 2. to damage somebody's reputation or good name.

**Despite**—regardless of, in spite of, insult or malice.

**Devour**—to destroy something rapidly, consume, demolish, overwhelm.

**Disciple**—1. one who is a follower or a student who learns from a teacher. 2. one who is forever learning. 3. in the Bible Jesus had twelve original followers or disciples whom He taught.

**Discipleship**—modeling and teaching the believers (Christians) the precepts of the Bible, prayer, the doctrine of Jesus, Christian living and worship.

**Discreet**—tactful, cautious, careful.

**Doctrine**—policy, principle, set of guidelines.

**Eloquent**—1. speaking or spoken beautifully and forcefully, expressive, and persuasive 2. expressing a feeling or thought clearly.

**Enmity**—the extreme ill will or hatred that exists between enemies.

**Entangled**—to involve somebody or something in a problem that will be difficult to escape from.

**Envy**—1. wanting what somebody else has, 2. to desire something possessed by somebody else.

**Epistle**—a letter written by the apostle Paul or other early Christian writers and included as a book of the Bible.

**Espoused**—a mutual promise or contract for a future marriage.

**Evangelist**—a person anointed and appointed by God to preach the gospel of Jesus Christ. Under the persuasive preaching of the Evangelist lost souls will come to Christ.

**Evil**—1. profoundly immoral or wrong, 2. harmful, deliberately causing great harm, pain or upset, 3. malicious, characterized by desire to cause hurt or harm, 4. Wicked.

**Evil Concupiscence**—morally bad, profoundly immoral or wrong—lust or strong feelings, powerful feelings of physical desire.

**Exhort**—1. urge to do something 2. to give warning or encouragement designed to motivate persons to action.

**Expedient**—appropriate, advisable, or useful in a situation that requires action.

**Faith**—1. Faith is to believe and trust God for those things that you have been praying for that is not visible to the eye will soon manifest. 2. Faith is what you don't see but you believe God for it to come to pass. 3. Faith is to believe God no matter what negative report they may give. Faith is no matter how sick you may be, I am going to believe God for my healing. 4. Faith is "I may be in between blessings but I am going to believe that my finances are going to line up with the word of God. 5. Faith is no matter how out of control my children may be, you believe God that my children will be saved, sanctified and living holy. 6. Faith is to believe God and not the system of the world.

**Flesh** —. The flesh is the earthly part of a person, representing lust and desires (Eph. 2:3). The flesh is contrary to the Spirit (Gal. 5:17). Those who are in the flesh cannot please God (Rom. 8:8). Well what do you mean in the flesh? I am a body. I am a person. How can I not be in the flesh? This statement is meaning not your skin or the meat on your body but to conduct yourself in ways that are contrary to the word of God. When a person is of the flesh they do things of this world. Such as lie, curse, drunk from alcohol or drugs, cheat, fornicate, backbite, steal and gossip. These are things that one would do because they have not yet been born of the Spirit of Christ. When you are born of the Spirit of Christ one would no longer do these things of the flesh. When one is of the flesh they take credit for everything that they do as a human being, the talent that I have, the education that I have, the knowledge that I have. It's all about my strength, and my ability. Those things also are all of the flesh because it was all about the individual and not about God.

**Forbearing**—to put up with, bear with or endure, to be patient, long suffering, forgiving and tolerant.

**Forbid**—prohibit, prevent, ban bar, outlaw or stop.

**Fornication**—sexual intercourse between two consenting adults who are not married to each other.

**Gentile**—a term used by Jewish people to refer to foreigners, or any other people who were not a part of the Jewish race.

**Gird**—1. get self ready, to prepare yourself for conflict or vigorous activity. 2. fasten something on. 3. restrain, fix, tighten.

**Glorify**—to magnify God through praising His name and honoring His commandments. Jesus also glorified His Father through His perfect obedience and His sacrificial death on our behalf.

**God**—1. 1. the creator and sustainer of the universe who has provided human mankind with a revelation of Himself through the natural world and through His Son, Jesus Christ. 2. Supernatural being, Deity, Spirit, Divinity.

**Gospel**—1. the Joyous good news of salvation in Jesus Christ. 2. the Greek word translated as gospel means a reward for bringing good news or simply good news.

**Grace**—Favor or kindness shown without regard to the worth or merit of the one who receives it and in spite of what that person deserves. Grace is one of the key attributes of God. This attribute of God is what moved Him to save us (unmerited favor). We realize that this refers to the fact that man did not deserve to be saved, but God made him the recipient of Salvation anyhow. Grace then refers to the act which Jesus performed in our stead. Although the grace of God is always free and undeserved, it must not be taken for granted. Grace is only enjoyed within the Covenant—the gift is given by God, and the gift is received by people through repentance and faith

**Hallowed**—holy to regard with great respect or reverence.

**Holy**—1. moral and ethical wholeness or perfection; freedom from moral evil. 2. holiness is one of the essential elements of God's nature required of His people. 3. holiness may also be rendered sanctification or godliness. 4. the Hebrew word for holy denotes that which is sanctified or set apart for divine service.

**Holy Ghost**—The Holy Ghost is the anointed and all powerful Spirit of Jesus Christ. The comforter which the Father sent back to all men everywhere all over this universe (John 14:26, Acts 2:38-39) after the ascension of Jesus. Our heavenly Father knew that we could not keep ourselves and that we would need a comforter so God sent the Holy Ghost. The Holy Ghost is the promise and a gift from God. The Holy Ghost is our source of spiritual power (Luke 12:12, 24:48-49, Acts 1:8, Rom 15:3). Without the Holy Ghost it is it's much harder to resist the devil and his temptation alone. Sanctification comes through the Holy Ghost (Rom. 15:16).

**Holy Spirit**—What is the Holy Spirit or the Spirit of God? The Spirit of God is *Wisdom, Understanding, and Knowledge* (Ex. 31:3, Ex. 35:31, Is. 11:2, and Dan. 2:21). Before the Holy Ghost came there always was and still is the Spirit of God for <u>every believer</u> (Gen. 1:2, John 7:37-39). The Spirit of God does not stop at the Old Testament but it goes all in to the New Testament. The Spirit of God didn't stop operating when Holy Ghost came. In the beginning there was the Spirit of God because the Holy Ghost was not yet given but the Holy Ghost and Holy Spirit are one of the same that work together for the <u>wholeness</u> of mankind everywhere.

The apostles were baptized in the *Holy Spirit* to enable them to execute their commission. The full gospel was officially preached and Jesus' last will and testament came into being, and the church became a reality, and remission of sin based on Jesus' shed blood was first experienced on the day of Pentecost when the Holy Ghost was received. This is what Acts 2:1 means when it says "when the day of Pentecost *was fully come.*

The Holy Ghost and Holy Spirit are not two but one. 1st John 5: 7 says "that there are three that bear record in heaven, the Father, the Word, and the Holy Ghost." We cannot take one interchangeable word (Ghost and Spirit) and make two. One of the operations is that the Spirit of God draws us to accept Christ and once we accept the Lord as our Savior, the spirit of God sustains us until we receive the Holy Ghost. John 6:44 says "No man can come to me except the Father which hath sent me draw him: and I will raise him up at the last day."

We did not come to Jesus on our own. It was the Spirit of God that drew us to Christ. We could not have come to Christ any other way. The Spirit of God was definitely upon us.

**Humble**—1. modest and unassuming in attitude and behavior, 2. feeling or showing respect toward other people.

**Hypocrite**—1. somebody who pretends to have admirable principles, beliefs, or feelings but behaves otherwise. 2. a fraud.

**Idolatry**—the worship of something created as opposed to the worship of the Creator Himself.

**Implacable**—impossible to pacify or to reduce in strength or force.

**Infidel**—1. somebody who does not believe in a major religion, especially Christianity. 2. a nonbeliever, somebody with no religious beliefs.

**Iniquity**—1. unrighteousness, lawlessness, wicked, evil, sin, injustice. 2. the Bible often uses this word to describe evil and wickedness. 3. iniquity can suggest different types of evil, such as transgressions of spiritual law and crimes against God.

**Inordinate Affection**—excessive love, undue love, unwarranted love.

**Inventors of Evil Things**—1. sexual explicit movies, adult toys, 2. anything, anyone, any game, any song that contributes to murder, violence and pre-marital sex.

**Jehovah El Elyon**—The Lord the Most High God

**Jehovah Elohim**—The Lord God of Gods'

**Jehovah Jireh**—The Lord Will Provide

**Jehovah Makkeh**—The Lord Our Judge

**Jehovah M'Kaddesh**—The Lord Our Sanctifier

**Jehovah Nissi**—The Lord is My Banner

**Jehovah Rapha**—The Lord is My Healer

**Jehovah Rohi**—The Lord Our Shepherd

**Jehovah Sabaoth**—The Lord of Host

**Jehovah Shalom**—The Lord of Peace

**Jehovah Shammah**—The Lord is there

**Jehovah Tsidkenu**—The Lord Our Righteousness

**Jesus**—1. Jehovah became salvation 2. Son of the living God born of a virgin. Our Savior, Our Redeemer 3. Jesus was the perfect one time sacrifice that came to this world to die so that you and I may live. Jesus died for our sins

**Justified**—1. justification is the process by which sinful human beings are made acceptable to a Holy God. 2. Being justified says that Jesus Christ has paid the penalty for our sins and what He did what no other human or animal could have done. 3. we are no longer guilty but we have been made free and vindicated through the blood o f Jesus Christ. 4. we are not guilty.

**Lasciviousness**—1. undisciplined and unrestrained behavior, especially a flagrant disregard of sexual restraints, 2. showing a desire for or unseemly interest in sex 3. erotic, provoking lust.

**Latchet**—Shoe strap

**Loins**—area between the ribs and the hips. 2. In the belt area.

**Longsuffering**—1. a word in the KJV and NKJV that refers primarily to God's patient endurance of the wickedness of the sinful. 2. The purpose to God's longsuffering is to lead the people to repentance.

**Lust**—1. desire for what is forbidden: an obsessive sexual craving. 2. the strong physical desire to have sex with somebody, usually without associated feelings of love or affection.

**Malice** or **Maliciousness**—1. the intention or desire to cause harm or pain to somebody. 2. hatred, spite, meanness, cruelty, wickedness.

**Malignity**—desire to do evil, intense hatred, strong desire to do harm or intentional harmful act.

**Mammon**—1. a word that speaks of wealth especially wealth that is used in opposition to God. 2. the personification of wealth portrayed as a false God. 3. wealth and riches considered as evil and corrupt influence.

**Mediator**—1. one who goes between two groups or persons to help them work out their differences and come to agreement. 2. A mediator can also be the negotiator of an agreement.

**Meekness**—1. an attitude of humility toward God and gentleness toward people, springing from a recognition that God is in control. 2. showing mildness or quietness of nature.

**Mercy**—1. gentleness, kindness, leniency, tenderness, compassion, considerate, 2. Easy going and slow to anger.

**Minister or Ministry**—1. to serve or to service. The model of this definition is Jesus who did not come to be served but to serve (Mk. 10:45). 2. Priest, preacher, clergy.

**Omnipotence**—God is All powerful. With God all things are possible (Matt. 19:26).

**Omnipresence**—God is not limited by space and time (Psalm.139:7-12).

**Omniscience**—this is the characteristic of God to know all things. There is no though conceived that He is not aware of (Psalm 139:1-6).

**Pagan**—a follower of a false god or a heathen religion; one who delights in sensual pleasures and material goods.

**Parable**—a short, simple story designed to communicate a spiritual truth, religious principle, or moral lesson; a figure of speech in which truth is illustrated by a comparison or example drawn from everyday experiences.

**Pastor**—1. one who leads a congregation of believers. 2. the under shepherd of the flock who is praying for the souls of the people. 3. the overseer of the church of God that feeds the people with knowledge and understanding. 4. a minister who has a congregation of people where he or she preaches and teaches the word of God.

**Pharaoh**—1. a ruler of ancient Egypt. 2. a powerful person. 3. somebody in position or authority especially somebody who is harsh, gives unreasonable orders and expects unquestioning obedience.

**Principalities**—1. powerful rulers or the rule of someone in authority. 2. This word is used in primarily in the bible as demonic spirits, angels and demons in general or any type of ruler other than God Himself.

**Prophecy**—to foretell the future or that which is to come. 2. divine prediction.

**Prophet**—the person who foretells the future or predicts a divine revelation.

**Propitiation**—The atoning death of Jesus on the cross, through which He paid the penalty demanded by God because of people's sin, thus setting them free from sin and death. Thus, propitiation expresses the idea that Jesus Died on the cross to pay the price for sin that a holy God demanded. Propitiation refers to the removal of that which is displeasing in one party so that the two can be brought together.

**Purloining**—to steal something especially when the theft breaks another's trust.

**Reconciliation**—The process by which God and people are brought together again. The bible teaches that we are alienated from God because of human sinfulness. Although God loves the sinner it is impossible for Him not to judge the sin (Rom.5:8 and He. 10:27).

**Redemption**—1. deliverance by payment of a price. 2. redemption refers to salvation from sin, death and the wrath of God by Christ's sacrifice. 3. Jesus paid for our redemption with His blood. 4. not the blood of animals but the precious blood of Jesus is what freed us from sin and bondage.

**Regeneration**—1. the spiritual change brought about in a person's life by an act of God. 2. in regeneration a person's sinful nature has been converted to the ways of unclean to clean and from unrighteousness to righteousness, from that of unholy to holy and from your own intellect to the mind of God.

**Remission**—1. release from sin. 2. the active nature of the word for remission in the Greek language indicates that forgiveness is more than a passive act.

**Repent**—1. to turn your back on sin. 2. to be sincerely sorry for your sin never to do it again. 3. to change your mind from the ways of the world to the ways and mind of Christ.

**Reprobate Mind**—at one time you were in church or you may still be in the church, you were hearing the word of God but the truth was falling on deaf ears. God was giving you a chance to change your mind (Repent) from your sinful ways of living to a mind to live for Him (God). You heard the word of God but refused to be ye transformed by the renewing of your mind (Rom. 12:2). You have strayed away from the truth. Because of your disobedience God is allowing you to listen to the false prophets, and those that have no knowledge or understanding of the word of God but think they do. Your way of thinking is not Godly nor is it rational. You are lying and repeating lies because this is now what you believe. You have been deceived by those who are informing you. But, your mind is so messed up from disobedience and rebellion against God you don't even know it. In your mind you think they **AND** you are right but you are just as wrong as two left shoes. You are quoting scriptures with no understanding and no meaning. You have been turned over to a reprobate mind by God. ( **PLEASE READ** 2<sup>nd</sup> **Thes. 2:9-12**, Rom. 1:18-32).

**Resurrection**—1. to be raised from the dead and never to die again. 2. this is when the Son of God was dead but He was raised from the dead by His Father. The word of God tells us that Jesus is the resurrection and the life, he that believeth in Him, though you were dead, yet shall you live (John 11:25). There have been others in the bible that was raised from the dead only to die again but not Jesus. Jesus Lives.

**Revel** or **Revellings**—1. to take great pleasure in something 2. to have an enjoyable time in the company of others, especially at parties. 3. drink, get drunk, paint the town red, wild parties.

**Revile**—1. to make a fierce or abusive verbal attack on somebody or something. 2. to use abusive or insulting language.

**Righteousness** —1. holy and upright living, in accordance with God's standard. 2. the word righteousness comes from a root word that means straightness. 3. righteousness is a moral concept. 4. God's character is the definition and source of all righteousness.

**Sacrifice**—1. the ritual through which the Hebrew people offered the blood or the flesh of an animal to God as a substitute payment for their sin. 2. a giving up of something valuable or important for somebody or something else considered to be of more value or importance.

**Salvation**—1. deliverance from the power of sin. 2. to be saved from damnation, hell and destruction.

**Sanctified**—1. to be set apart from that which is dirty to that which is clean, from that which is unholy to that which is holy, from that which is unrighteous to that which is righteous 2. the process of God's grace by which the believer is separated from sin and becomes dedicated to God's righteousness.

**Saved**—to confess with your mouth and believe in your heart that Jesus is Lord.

**Savior**—1. a person who rescues others from evil, danger, or destruction and in this case His name is Jesus. Jesus is our only personal Savior. 2. Jesus our Savior rescued us from sin so that we may be saved.

**Scythian**—a barbaric race that lived in Scythia, an ancient region of southeastern Europe and southwestern Asia now generally identified as Russia.

**Servant**—1. one who works for the Lord. 2. one who ministers and serves the people of God.

**Servile**—1. too willing to agree with somebody or to do anything, however demeaning, that somebody wants. 2. relating to slaves or condition of slavery.

**Sin**—1. an act, thought, or way of behaving that goes against the law or teachings of a religion especially when the person who commits it is aware of it. 2. something that offends a moral or ethical principle. 3. lawlessness (1st John 3:4) or transgression of God's will, either by omitting to do what God's law requires or by doing what it forbids. 4. the transgression can occur in thought word or deed.

**Sinner**—1. one who goes against the laws of God. 2. one who commits acts of thoughts, deeds, or behaviors that is totally against the nature of God.

**Smote**—to strike or to hit hard

**Sober**—marked by self control; of sound moral judgment.

**Sojourning** —1. a short stay at a place. 2. to stay at a place for a time.

**Sow**—to scatter or plant seed on an area of land in order to grow crops.

**Spiritual Adoption**—Adoption is the act of voluntarily accepting responsibility of a child. The term adoption as used in the New Testament means "placing as son." It is found in the New Testament five times. The term is used with reference to rights and privileges.

When Man was created he obtained certain rights and privileges. He has dominion over God's vineyard, he moved without fear or harm, he communed freely and fearlessly with God. When man sinned these privileges were cut off. He surrendered his rights as a child of God. We are the children of Adam by nature. Our rights to eternal life therefore were lost.

By the spirit of adoption we become the children of God and have and this gives us the right to call him Father. When we receive His Spirit we are restored to full rights and privileges as sons. Communion with God is restored; accessibility to His protection and help is ours by right. We are heirs of God, joint heirs with Christ in the kingdom and power of God.

**Subtle**—1. slight and not obvious 2. intelligent, experienced, or sensitive enough to make refined judgments and distinctions.

**Suffice**—1. to be enough, 2. to meet expected requirements.

**Supplication**—1. a humble and sincere appeal to somebody who has the power to grant a request.2. the addressing of humble and sincere appeals to somebody with the power to grant them. 3. prayer, request, plea.

**Tares**—1. a poisonous grass resembling wheat, but with smaller seeds. 2. the tares were usually left in the fields until harvest time, then separated from the wheat during winnowing.

**Teacher**—1. one who instructs and or imparts knowledge 2. teaching is to be distinguished from preaching, the gospel. 3. teaching in the Christian faith was validated by Jesus, who was called a Teacher more than anything else.

**Temperance**—1. control over sensual desires. 2. the meaning of the word temperate is to have self control that masters all kinds of sensual desires. 3.through temperance Christians can discipline body and spirit, so that they are more capable of striving for their spiritual reward.

**Temptation**—1. an enticement or invitation to sin, with the implied promise of greater good to be derived from following the way of disobedience. 2. God does not tempt people, nor can He Himself as the holy God be tempted (James 1:13). 3. a desire or craving for something, especially something considered wrong.

**Transform**—to change radically in inner character, condition, or nature.

**Transgression** —1. the violation of a law, command, or duty. 2. the Hebrew word most often translated as transgression in the Old Testament means revolt or rebellion. 3. in the Greek translation it means to deliberately breech the laws of God.

**Unclean, Uncleanness**—defiled, foul, unfit.

P A S T O R  L O R E T T A  R O R I E

**Ungodly**—1. to go against the laws and nature of God. 2. sinful, and wicked.

**Unmerciful**—no compassion, no kindness, or not willing to forgive.

**Vigilant**—1. watchful and alert, especially to guard against danger. 2. attentive, alert, cautious, observant and on your guard.

**Vile Affections**—disgusting feelings, wicked feelings, and extremely unpleasant feelings.

**Wickedness**—1.evil, very wrong or very bad. 2. sin, iniquity and malice.

**Wiles**—1. cunning behavior intended to persuade somebody to do something. 2. to trick or entice somebody. 3. Deceit.

**Without Natural Affection**—when you have affection for the same gender as yourself (totally against the nature of God).

**Wrath**—1. the personal manifestation of God's holy moral character in judgment against sin. 2. It is no way vindictive or malicious. 3. It is holy indignation God's anger directed against sin.

**Yokefellow**—the word implies one who is yoked in harness with another—the two working as a team.

**Zeal** or **Zealous**—1. enthusiastic devotion; eager desire. 2. passionate and obsessive.